More Telescope Power

More Telescope Power

All New Activities and Projects for Young Astronomers

GREGORY L. MATLOFF

with drawings by C. Bangs

John Wiley & Sons, Inc.

This book is printed on acid-free paper. ♾

Published by John Wiley & Sons, Inc., New York
Published simultaneously in Canada

Illustrations by C. Bangs
Figures 1.2, 3.3, and 6.1 courtesy of NASA
Figures 4.2, 6.2, 6.3, 6.4A, 6.5B, 6.5, and 6.6 courtesy of NASA/JPL/CalTech
Figures 5.3 and 5.4 courtesy of Solar and Heliospheric Observatory (SOHO). SOHO is a project of international cooperation between ESA and NASA.

The publisher and the author have made every reasonable effort to ensure that the experiments and activities in the book are safe when conducted as instructed but assume no responsibility for any damage caused or sustained while performing the experiments or activities in this book. Parents, guardians, and/or teachers should supervise young readers who undertake the experiments and activities in this book.

Library of Congress Cataloging-in-Publication Data:

Matloff, Gregory L.
More telescope power : all new activities and projects for young astronomers / Gregory L. Matloff ; with drawings by C. Bangs.
p. cm.
Includes index.
Summary: Presents various astronomy activities using a telescope, including constructing a simple telescope, tracking satellites, and sketching details of the moon.
ISBN 0-471-40985-5 (pbk. : alk. paper)
1. Telescopes—Experiments—Juvenile literature. 2. Astronomy—Experiments—Juvenile literature. [1. Telescopes—Experiments. 2. Astronomy—Experiments. 3. Experiments.] I. Bangs, Constance, ill. II. Title.

QB88 .M379 2001
522'.2'078—dc21 2001046738

Printed in the United States of America

10 9 8 7 6 5 4 3 2 1

Jupiter shall emerge, be patient, watch again
another night, the Pleiades shall emerge,
They are immortal, all those stars both silvery and
golden shall shine out again.
The great stars and the little ones shall shine
out again, they endure,
The vast immortal suns and the long-enduring
pensive moons shall again shine.

—Walt Whitman, "On the Beach at Night,"
Year of Meteors (1859–1860)

Contents

6 ★ The Planets 61

7 ★ The Stars 81

Introduction: Tools of the Astronomer

Humans have wondered about the sky for thousands of years. This celestial curiosity may be one of the things that distinguishes us from other life-forms. Yet for most of human history, our means of investigating celestial objects were defined by our limitations, not our capabilities.

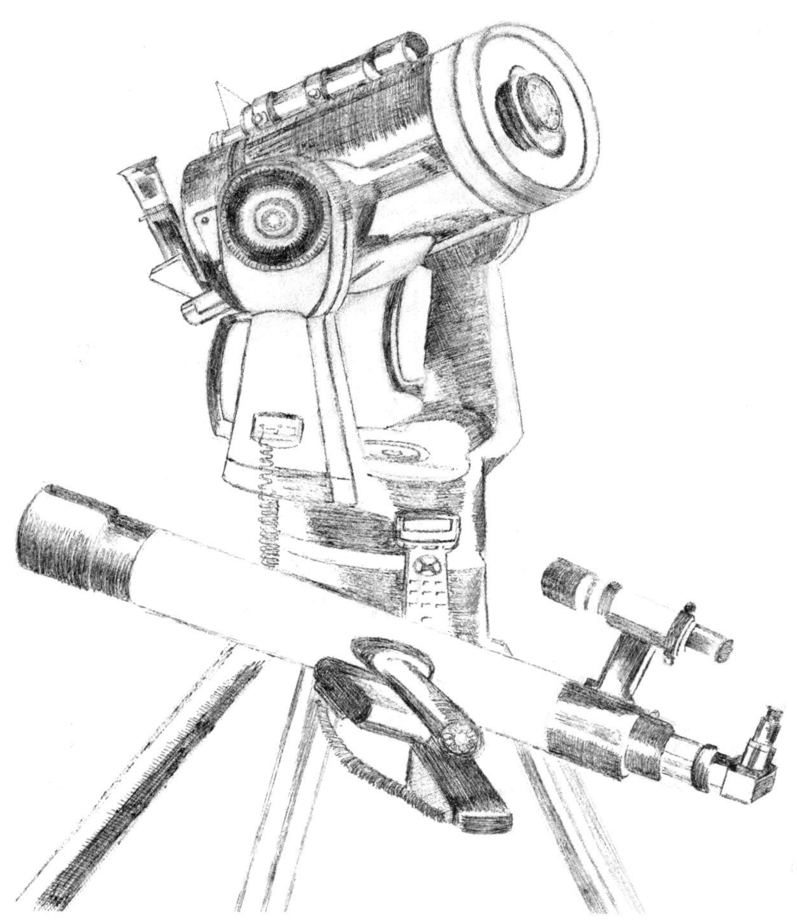

Limitations of Early Astronomers

The first limitation experienced by early astronomers was that of nature—we live at the bottom of an ocean of air that renders astronomical observations difficult. Cloudy skies block all light from celestial objects, and the gases and particles in the atmosphere block some light, especially in certain colors of the spectrum. Even through the clearest skies, celestial objects can be viewed from the ground only at certain times. In the twenty-first century, the proximity of artificial light makes it harder to see dim stars.

In spite of these problems, people have known since before the dawn of history that some celestial objects—the stars—seem to be steadfast and arranged in regular sky patterns. Other objects—the Moon, the Sun, and planets—change in appearance and in their position in the skies. Early astronomers were fascinated by the regularities and motions of the celestial objects.

In Bronze Age Britain, astronomer-priests kept track of the rising and setting of the Sun and the Moon by sighting through circular arrangements of stones, such as Stonehenge; Babylonian astrologers of 1000 B.C. observed planetary motions from the top of large towers called *ziggurats*. Around 500 B.C., Greek astronomers constructed the first crude models of planetary motions and attempted to estimate the relative brightness of visible stars.

But all these efforts were limited by available technology. The only existing detector of skylight was the human eye. Early observing tools, such as alignments of rocks or similar pointers, could help determine lunar phases and motions, solar motions, and variations in planetary position, but not much more.

An Astronomical Revolution

Approximately four centuries ago, a technological advance led to a great increase in our understanding of celestial objects. Astronomers such as Galileo Galilei (1564–1642) began for the first time to use arrangements of lenses (and later, mirrors) to magnify the size of celestial objects, making dim objects seem brighter and increasing the amount of detail visible on the surfaces of our neighbors in the solar system.

The earliest telescopes were constucted using an arrangement of lenses like the one shown in Figure I-1. Light from a distant source, such as a star, arrives at the objective lens. The *objective lens* bends the light rays so that they all meet at a point called the *focus*. The distance between a lens and its focus is called the *focal length*. The *eyepiece* lens is arranged so that its focus corresponds with that of the objective lens, as shown. When you look through the eyepiece, you see a magnified image of the object. This kind of telescope is called a *refracting telescope* because the light rays are *refracted* (bent) when they pass through the

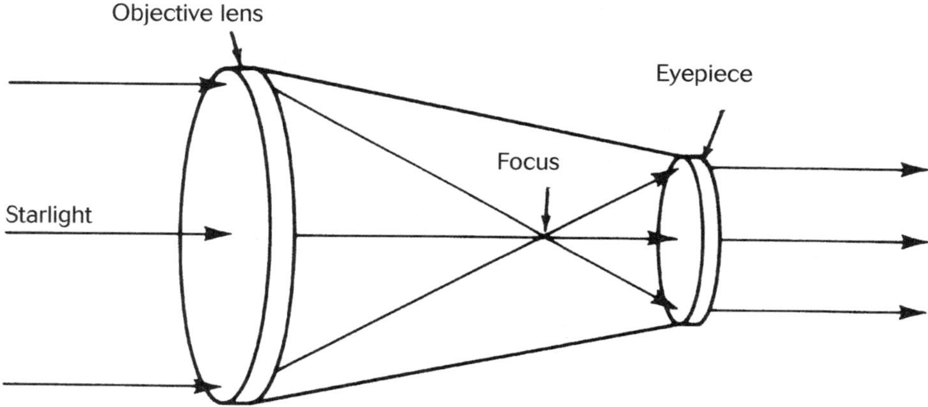

Figure I-1. A *simple refracting telescope.*

objective lens. After they pass through the focus, the light rays diverge, or draw apart, until they encounter the eyepiece, which projects them to the observer's eye. The image of a celestial object viewed through a telescope is inverted, or upside down. In a *reflecting telescope,* a curved *primary mirror* replaces the objective lens (see Figure I-2). The effective diameter of the objective lens or primary mirror is called the *aperture.*

Of course, not all telescopes are alike. Astronomers characterize and compare their telescopes using four quantities: magnification, field of view, light-gathering power, and resolution.

Magnification defines how much larger the image of a small, distant object is made by a telescope. This quantity is defined as the ratio of objective focal length (or primary-mirror focal length in a reflecting telescope) to eyepiece focal length, or f_{obj} / f_{eye}. Let's say that your objective focal length is 20 mm and your eyepiece focal length is 10 mm. Your telescope will have a magnification of 2×.

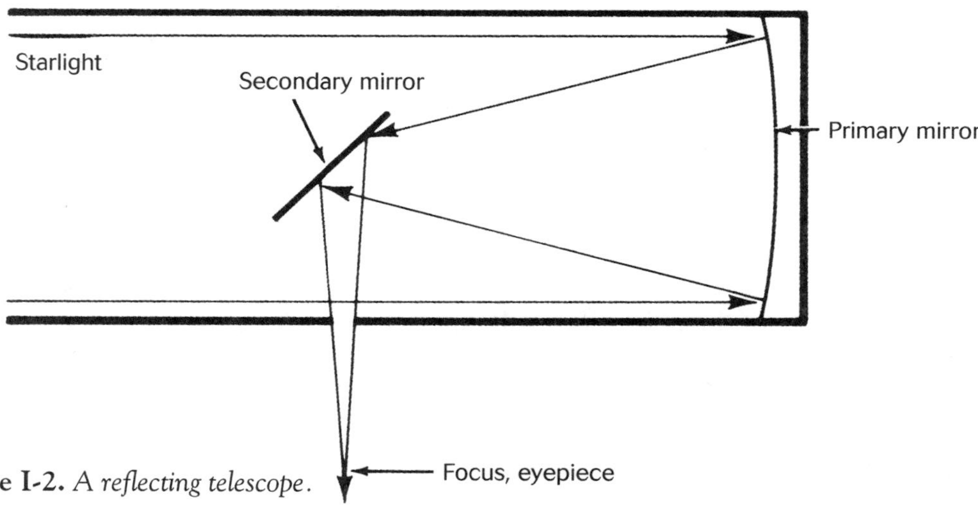

Figure I-2. A *reflecting telescope.*

A telescope's *field of view (FOV)* is the angular fraction of the night sky that can be viewed through your eyepiece. One penalty of very high magnifcation is very small FOV.

Light-gathering power (LGP) is a measure of how much brighter a dim distant object appears when viewed through the eyepiece of your telescope. A telescope's LGP depends upon the area of the objective lens (or the primary mirror in a reflecting telescope). The relative area is found by squaring the diameter of the objective lens or primary mirror. For example, a 10-cm-diameter telescope has four times the area of a 5-cm telescope and 4× the light-gathering power. Therefore, a star will be four times brighter when viewed through the larger instrument.

Resolution, or *resolving power*, is the ability of your telescope to help you discriminate fine details of the celestial objects you observe, such as the craters of the Moon and cloud bands of Jupiter. Resolution increases with increasing telescope aperture (a 10-cm aperture telescope has twice the resolution of a 5-cm instrument). Resolution is better for blue light than for red.

Telescope Evolution and Accessories

After several centuries of telescope use, many improvements have been made to the instrument. We have binoculars (double refractors that use additional optics to produce right-side-up images), several types of reflectors, and hybrid reflector/refractors. Consult my previous book, *Telescope Power* (Wiley, 1993), for more information on telescope varieties.

Many telescopes are equipped with electrical clock drives that allow you to compensate for the motion of the Earth and view celestial objects for many minutes. A host of accessories—planispheres, filters, eyepieces, and spectroscopes—are marketed to both professional and amateur astronomers.

The *planisphere* is an inexpensive, handheld device that can be adjusted for date, time, and sometimes, location, to present the configuration of the brighter stars in the night sky. Simple planispheres can be purchased at low cost from your local planetarium or science museum. You may also wish to consult the pages of *Astronomy* and *Sky & Telescope* magazines for monthly sky maps. Many local "sky maps" can also be downloaded from the World Wide Web.

Color *filters* are also available. These are generally designed to screw on to telescope eyepieces and allow you to partially compensate for light pollution, reduce the glare of the full Moon, and improve the color contrast of some celestial objects. Other filters, as well as special eyepieces, are described in detail in *Telescope Power*.

The spectroscope is a useful tool for analyzing the color of celestial objects. Our eyes receive "white light" from celestial objects, which is a combination of all colors radiated. A *spectroscope* is an instrument that separates this received electromagnetic energy into its various colors. We can study the different colors emitted by celestial objects to learn about their temperature and composition.

In recent decades, another astronomical revolution has allowed some astronomers to overcome the sky-seeing limitations imposed by increased urbanization. These lucky few have been able to observe from platforms such as the Hubble Space Telescope and the Chandra X-ray Observatory, which are located in space far above the Earth's atmosphere. Instruments such as these have revealed new elements of the structure of the universe, provided detailed images of star-forming regions across the universe, and obtained evidence for the existence of mysterious cosmic objects, such as black holes and dark matter.

Although most astronomers will not have the opportunity to use these sophisticated space observatories, the results from these instruments are usually posted on the World Wide Web. Earth-bound astronomers can also view large space observatories, and other artificial satellites such as space shuttles and space stations, using their backyard telescopes.

★1★

The Many Satellites of Earth

In a fraction of a second, some of these orbiting objects beam our voices around the world. Others help us track the weather, study climatic changes, and assist with military intelligence. Some of the most exciting serve as temporary homes to small groups of humans or carry various instruments that help us peer into the farthest recesses of the universe. They are Earth's artificial *satellites*.

As a teenager during the then-new space age in the early 1960s, I can well remember the thrill of searching the skies with my first telescope for a glimpse of one of the earliest of these objects. Most of them looked like moving stars even under moderate magnification, but I can never forget my excitement when I resolved the spherical shape of an Echo balloon satellite as it orbited a few hundred kilometers above my head.

A Short History of the Early Space Age

The first artificial Earth satellite, *Sputnik 1*, was successfully launched into orbit by Russia in October 1957. Since that time, thousands of spacecraft have been launched into space—most into *low Earth orbit* (LEO), a few hundred kilometers above Earth's surface. Without specialized viewing equipment, the smaller of the LEO satellites are invisible, as are the satellites in higher orbits or those that have escaped the Earth's gravitational influence.

But even the unassisted eye can detect larger spacecraft in LEO, such as space shuttles and space stations. And binoculars or small telescopes can even resolve details of these large spacecraft.

ACTIVITY 1-1

Observing Satellites in Low Earth Orbit

Many American and Western European low-orbit satellites are in near-equatorial orbits, traveling from west to east at about 8 km/sec. This is because the Earth *rotates* (spins about its axis) from west to east at about 0.5 km/sec, as measured at the equator. In equatorial west–east orbits, the Earth's rotation means that less fuel is required for a satellite to acheive orbit. Russian launch sites, on the other hand, are at high latitudes and satellites launched from these locations often pass over Earth's poles. Although such near-polar north–south orbits are less economical, they have the advantage of passing over all of the Earth's surface.

Your local newspaper, television station, or the NASA web site (http://www.nasa.gov) will tell you when a large satellite is expected to make a visible pass over your location. Like the Moon, satellites shine because of reflected sunlight, so they are only visible when sunlight reflects off them in your direction. You will need a magnetic compass to help locate the satellite's visible track because its location is usually reported in compass directions. Since the duration of a visible satellite pass is only a few minutes, you will have to move your binoculars or telescope rapidly to keep the spacecraft in your field of view. The duration of a satellite's visible pass depends upon satellite height and structure and the Sun's altitude in the sky.

A satellite's orbit is its *trajectory*, or path, around the Earth. The Earth's gravitational force keeps artificial satellites, as well as Earth's natural satellite—the Moon, in orbit. The least amount of rocket fuel is required to launch a satellite into a circular low orbit about the Earth. More fuel is required to achieve higher orbits or to escape from the Earth's gravitational influence. The Earth's gravitational field works as if all of our planet's mass, or total amount of material, is concentrated at the center. A satellite therefore orbits around the Earth's center, not around its surface.

Without getting too involved in higher mathematics, there are a number of tools for considering the principles of spacecraft trajectories. One of the most graphic of these is the concept of conic sections.

Orbits and Conic Sections

The *conic section* was developed by ancient Greek mathematicians who were interested in pure mathematics, not applications. One of the pioneers in this field was Apollonius of Perga, who lived in the third century B.C.

To make a conic section, first construct a cone out of cardboard. The base of the cone is a circle, the apex (top) is a point. As shown in Figure 1-1, a cut across the cone parallel to the base will generate a circle. If you cut at a slight angle to the base, you will have a stretched circle, or an ellipse. More extreme cuts result in parabolas and hyperbolas. A *parabola* is a curve that is open at one end. No matter how far out you draw it, the ends will never close. A *hyperbola* is even more divergent from a circle.

In a circular orbit, the satellite is always the same distance from Earth's center. It travels around the Earth at a constant velocity (speed).

Most satellites are in elliptical orbits around the Earth's center. At the high point of an elliptical orbit (called the *apogee*), when the satellite is farthest from Earth, the satellite moves slower than at its lowest point, or *perigee*, when it is closest to Earth.

Unlike circles and ellipses, parabolas and hyperbolas are open curves. A spacecraft that has just escaped the Earth's gravitational influence moves along

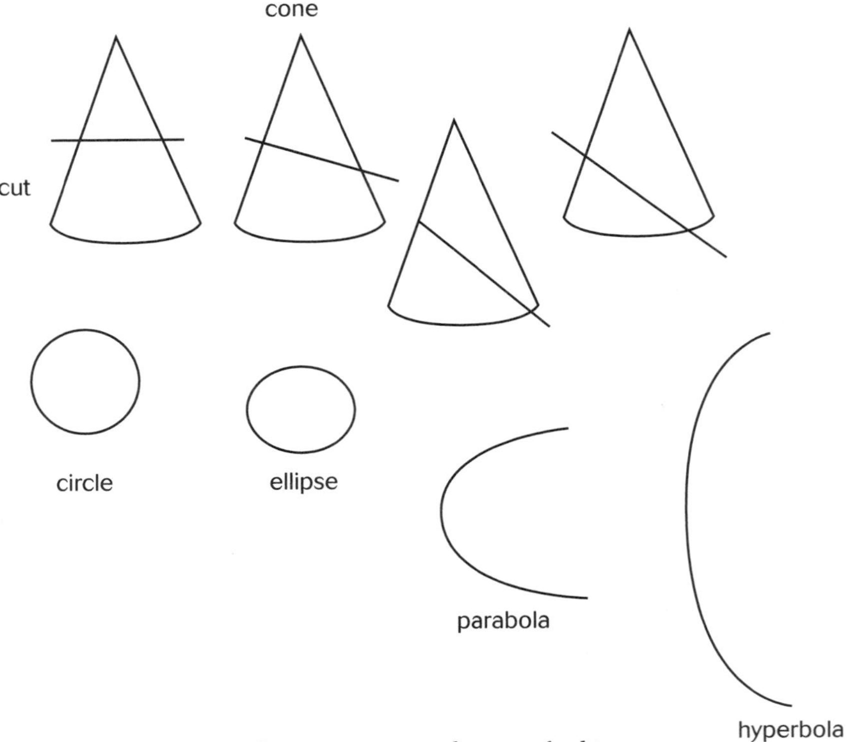

Figure 1-1. *Conic sections and types of orbits.*

a parabolic track, rather than in a closed orbit. Most interplanetary spacecraft are moving along hyperbolic paths relative to the Earth, but are still in closed circular or elliptical orbits around the Sun.

Acceleration, Mass, and Force

Two concepts that are important in the understanding of gravity and orbits are mass and acceleration. *Acceleration* is the rate at which an object's velocity changes. The *velocity* of an object is the distance it covers in a specified time interval. When an object is dropped from a tower near Earth's surface, the acceleration of gravity (called *g*) is 9.8 m per square second. This means that, if the initial velocity of the object is zero, it is falling at a velocity of 9.8 m/sec after one second, 19.6 m/sec after two seconds, and so on (disregarding the effects of air resistance).

Mass (denoted by *m*) is the amount of material within a body. The more mass an object has, the greater its *inertia*, or resistance to changes of motion. You can easily throw a low-mass marble across the room, but try that with a high-

Galileo vs. Aristotle: Battle of the Titans

Our understanding of how satellites are launched into orbit began with the intellectual battle of two titans of human thought. In one corner was Aristotle, a great Greek philosopher of the fourth century B.C. His opponent was Galileo, the sixteenth-century Italian scientist who first applied the telescope to astronomy.

Both of these men investigated gravity in an attempt to understand how things fall toward the center of the Earth when dropped from a height. Historians believe that Aristotle may have considered objects with different shapes as well as different masses. When he dropped, say, a low-mass piece of papyrus and a high-mass rock, the more massive rock fell at a faster rate. Not realizing that air resistance would slow the fall of the papyrus (as it reduces the velocity of a descending parachute), Aristotle incorrectly concluded that the more massive an object was, the more rapid its descent when the object was dropped from a height.

Galileo conducted similar experiments, but he used similiarly shaped objects so that the effects of air resistance were reduced. He concluded correctly that when objects of different masses are released in a gravity field such as the Earth's, the rate of descent of each object is a constant that is independent of the object's mass. In other words, two objects of the same size but different weights released simultaneously from the same height above the ground would both fall at the same rate and hit the ground at the same time. Many of Galileo's experiments were performed publicly and observed by many people, although there is no proof that he actually dropped balls of different mass from the Leaning Tower of Pisa.

mass object such as your family car. You can't throw the car because it has more inertia than the marble.

Your weight is an example of a *force*—the product of mass and acceleration. Your weight is defined by the product mg, where m is your mass and g is the Earth's gravitational acceleration near the surface of our planet. If m is measured in kilograms and g is in meters per square second, then weight is calculated in a unit called newtons.

Gravity and Orbits

Sir Isaac Newton (1642–1727), an English scientist, considered gravity to be a force between objects that is always attractive. In Newton's theory of gravity, the gravitational field produced by a massive body acts as if all the mass of the body is concentrated at its center.

Newton demonstrated that a moving object's inertia will tend to maintain the object on a straight-line path at constant velocity. The Earth's gravitational field will tend to pull the object back toward the ground.

If a rocket is launched from the Earth at low velocity, gravity wins and the rocket will fall back to Earth. If it is launched with a very high velocity (greater than 11 km/sec), inertia wins and the rocket escapes the Earth's gravitational field into orbit around the Sun. But at a velocity of 8 km/sec and a height within a few hundred kilometers of Earth's surface, inertia and gravity balance out. The rocket becomes an artificial satellite, endlessly "falling" in a closed orbit around the Earth.

The velocity of an Earth-orbiting satellite slowly decreases as orbital height is increased. In a circular low orbit at a height of a few hundred kilometers above the Earth's surface, the orbital velocity is about 8 km/sec. If the satellite is raised to a circular orbit 6,000 km above Earth's surface, the orbital velocity falls to about 5.7 km/sec.

ACTIVITY 1-2

Estimating the Velocity of a Satellite in LEO

You should first set up your telescope with a low-power eyepiece, since this size eyepiece has a relatively large field of view (FOV). A large FOV will allow you to track the satellite for a longer time.

To estimate your eyepiece's FOV, first focus on the Moon. The Moon subtends (covers) an angle of about 0.5°. (There are 360° of arc in a closed circle. In each degree, there are 60 smaller angular divisions called minutes, and each minute has 60 seconds.) If the full Moon fills half your eyepiece, your telescope's eyepiece has an FOV of 1°. If the Moon fills one-quarter of the eyepiece, the FOV is 2°.

Once you have determined your telescope's FOV, you can estimate a LEO satellite's orbital velocity by recording how long it is within your telescope's FOV. In every orbit, a satellite in LEO circles the Earth and travels about 6.3 times the radius of the Earth, or about 40,000 km. During this time, it covers 360° since it is completing one circular orbit.

Let's say that your telescope's FOV is 1°. If you time how many seconds it takes the satellite to move through your scope's FOV and multiply by 360, you will get the time it takes the satellite to complete one orbit. If you divide this time in seconds into 40,000 km, you will have estimated the satellite's orbital velocity in kilometers per second.

For example, if the satellite takes 90 minutes, or 5,400 seconds, to orbit the Earth, then its circular orbital velocity is about 40,000/5,400, or 7.5 km/sec. If the orbit of the satellite is elliptical rather than circular, your results will be an approximation. Satellites in elliptical orbit slow down when farthest from the Earth and speed up when closest.

ACTIVITY 1-3

Can You See Any Detail on a Large Satellite in LEO?

Once you have mastered tracking a satellite through a low-power eyepiece, you might wish to change to a higher-power eyepiece.

With practice, you should be able to change eyepieces from low to high magnification while a large low-orbiting satellite is traveling through your telescope's FOV. Under good lighting conditions, you may be able to see the wings of a space shuttle or the solar panels of a space station.

Figure 1-2. *The space shuttle* Atlantis *approaching the Russian Space Station* Mir.

Geosynchronous Orbits

Although most spacecraft launched from Earth are in low Earth orbit, there are other significant orbital locations. Some satellites hang in much higher *geosynchronous Earth orbit* (GEO). In a geosynchronous orbit above the Earth's equator, a satellite circles the Earth every 24 hours. It will therefore seem to remain stationary in the sky.

A GEO satellite must be situated in a circular orbit at a height of about 36,000 km. At such a height, the satellite's orbital velocity is about 3 km/sec.

Communication satellites serving the United States and most of Western Europe are in GEO. When your long-distance telephone call is routed through one of these robotic outposts, you will notice a time lag in the conversation. This is because radio is a form of *electromagnetic radiation*, which is propagated by variations in electric or magnetic fields, and therefore moves at the speed of light (300,000 km/sec). A half-second time delay is introduced when your question to your distant friend travels up to the satellite and back again and your friend's answer performs the same journey in reverse.

Most amateur astronomers do not attempt to observe geosynchronous satellites because of the vast distances involved. But in a letter printed in the January 2000 issue of *Sky & Telescope*, Jim and Karen Young describe how observations of large GEO satellites can be accomplished. You will need a 15-to-25-cm telescope aperture, a high-quality telescope mount, a dark observing site, good knowledge of the equatorial sky, and a whole lot of patience to see these distant craft.

Other Satellite Observations

During the early 1970s, a few experiments were perfomed aboard spacecraft leaving the Earth that could be viewed even by naked-eye observers. As shown in the movie *Apollo 13*, urine was dumped overboard by some Apollo craft en route to the Moon just after departing LEO. The urine droplets crystallized into a bright, fuzzy star that could be viewed for minutes and resulted in a number of UFO reports.

The purpose of this experiment was to investigate gas diffusion in the space environment. Similiar experiments are conducted today when visible particle clouds are released at high altitudes by rockets to observe high-altitude winds. These experiments are usually announced by NASA in advance, and amateur astronomers are encouraged to participate.

As a satellite in low orbit moves around the Earth, it encounters occasional atoms of atmospheric gas. The resulting drag causes the satellite's orbit to eventually decay unless rockets are used to compensate. Small LEO satellites burn up as they enter Earth's atmosphere. The luminous tracks of dying satellites provide dramatic sky shows. Portions of large satellites may survive to reach our planet's surface.

THE END OF *MIR*

On March 23, 2001, the veteran Russian space station *Mir* was successfully de-orbited (brought out of orbit) over the South Pacific Ocean. Controllers from the ground crew directed *Mir's* final moments so that atmospheric drag would not cause the massive (140,000-kg) craft to descend over populated areas. *Mir* was launched in 1986 and had long since exceeded its designed life-span.

The fall of *Mir* was visible to amateur astronomers on the island of Fiji. The most spectacular views were obtained from three aircraft chartered to carry observers into the *Mir* crash zone.

Mir was observed to break up into eight distinct fireballs. Observers on the Fiji beach also reported a smoke trail left by the descending craft and a sonic boom as large components of *Mir* encountered the lower atmosphere. It is unclear how much of the massive space station survived to splash down into the Pacific Ocean.

But satellites are not the only celestial objects to be influenced by Earth's atmosphere. Meteors, or "shooting stars," are produced when tiny interplanetary ice or dust grains enter Earth's atmosphere. We'll look at some of these in the next chapter.

★2★

Dust Grains from Heaven

When talking about celestial bodies that enter Earth's atmosphere, we first must clear up a somewhat confusing terminology. A *meteor*, also known as a "shooting star," is a tiny particle of ice or dust, usually from a comet's tail, that burns up in Earth's upper atmosphere.

Much larger are *meteorites*, which are bodies from space that are large enough to survive passage through the Earth's atmosphere and hit the surface of our planet. Meteorites are thought to originate from asteroids and the solid parts of comets, and are displayed in many science and natural history museums.

A *meteoroid* is a meteor or meteorite before it encounters Earth's atmosphere. About 65 million years ago, a meteoroid from an asteroid or comet entered the Earth's atmosphere. This object measured in the neighborhood of 10 km across. When it hit the Earth, the impact had the force of thousands of hydrogen bombs exploding at the same time and in the same place. It was intense enough to change Earth's climate and destroy the dinosaurs and many

Asteroids

An *asteroid* is a chunk of mostly solid material left over from the formation of the solar system. There are three basic types of asteroids based on their composition: stony, rocky, and carbon-rich.

Most asteroids reside in a broad region within the solar system called the asteroid belt, which extends roughly from the orbit of Mars to that of Jupiter. Typical members of the asteroid belt never approach the Earth closer than hundreds of millions of kilometers. Although Hollywood's science fiction epics such as *Star Wars* depict asteroid belts as crowded places, they are actually quite empty. At least four robotic ships from Earth (*Pioneer 10* and *11* and *Voyager 1* and *2*) have successfully traversed the solar system's asteroid belt without experiencing any impacts. There are many thousands of large asteroids (up to a few hundred kilometers across) and perhaps millions of small ones (with sizes of 100 m or smaller) in the asteroid belt, but this region takes up an awful lot of space!

Some asteroids, however, are not confined to the main belt. Some solar system planets, notably giant Jupiter, have bunches of asteroidal objects following or leading them in their orbits. These asteroids are called the Trojans, named after heroes of the Trojan War from Homer's *Iliad* and *Odyssey*.

Other asteroids have been captured as satellites by various solar-system planets. A third class, called the near Earth asteroids, may venture closer to the Sun than our planet's orbit. Some of these have been noted to approach the Earth within a few hundred thousand kilometers. Collisions or gravitational interaction with giant planets may have driven these asteroids into the inner solar system.

Telescopes on the Earth and in space have revealed that some asteroids are accompanied by satellites—smaller asteroids that orbit them. Meteoroids may originate from asteroidal collisions or by disruptions in the solar orbits of asteroids by giant planets.

other terrestrial life-forms. Scientists have detected the eroded remnants of the impact crater from this event in Yucatán, Mexico. This crater must have originally been more than 100 kilometers across.

Comets

Comets are best pictured as celestial icebergs. Far from the Sun, the rocky nuclei (cores) of comets are coated with layers of dust and icy ammonia, methane, and water. Most comets orbit the Sun at distances of billions or trillions of kilometers. Alignments of giant planets or passing stars occasionally push some comets sunward.

Although perhaps only 20 km in size in the frozen outer reaches of the solar system, comets greatly expand when they approach the sun as the ice melts and evaporates. Comet tails may be 100,000,000 km in length and are produced by the pressure of sunlight on the evaporated gas clouds surrounding the comet's nucleus. (See Chapter 4 for hints on comet viewing.)

Types of Meteors

Although it is very unliklely that you will witness the fall of a meteorite, you may notice 10 or more meteor trails during a night's observing session. There are at least two types of meteors that are commonly observed. Most observations are of ordinary meteors, tiny dust or ice grains from comet tails that burn up in Earth's upper atmosphere. Most meteors have a pre-entry mass of about 1 g and can be measured in millimeters. Meteors appear at a height of 100 to 150 km above the Earth's surface and burn out at heights as low as 50 km.

If the meteoroid has a mass of many grams, however, it will produce a longer and brighter track as it disintegrates in Earth's upper atmosphere. These much rarer but more dramatic sky displays are called *bolides* or fireballs. Some bolides are brighter than the full Moon and may be visible in daylight. The luminous trail of a bolide may persist for minutes until high-altitude winds disperse it. The upper-air explosions that accompany the demise of a bolide are sometimes audible from the ground. The book of Joshua in the Bible may mention the fall and explosion of a bolide in the description of the "Sun standing still" over Gibeon; bolides may have been observed by Alexander's army more than 2,000 years ago while on campaign in Asia.

The Origin of Meteors

Some meteors are sporadic events and others occur in predictable periodic showers. The vast majority of these objects originate from comets and asteroids. A tiny fraction of collected meteorites originate from impacts or very ancient volcanic eruptions on the Moon or Mars, which throw off material that eventually reaches the Earth.

Many of the meteroids that become bolides or sporadic meteors probably began their careers as near Earth asteroids. But very rare collisions between asteroids in the asteroid belt and gravitational influences of the giant planets can also serve to direct some small asteroidal bodies earthward.

Most periodic meteors, on the other hand, result when tiny dust and ice particles are evaporated from the nuclei of a comet as the comet is heated during close solar approaches. These tiny meteoroids spread out along the orbit of the comet as a diffuse dust ring circling the Sun. Twice each year, when the Earth on its orbit intersects the comet's trajectory, a meteor shower of dozens of meteors per hour can be observed at predictable dates and locations.

The parent cometary body for most meteor showers is known to experts. The approximate duration of each meteor storm is also predictable. What is not known in advance is the intensity of a meteor shower. Careful observation is required to determine the number of meteors per hour, the average length and duration of the meteor track, and whether any exciting bolides can be observed in conjunction with a periodic meteor shower.

Observing Meteors

A large telescope is overkill in meteor observation. A small pair of binoculars or even the unassisted eye is more than ample. You will also need a comfortable chair, a watch with a second hand, a magnetic compass to orient you with the magnetic north pole, a notebook and writing implements, and a red-tinted flashlight (because red light has the least effect on your night vision). It also helps to have a few friends along to help you record the length and number of meteor tracks that your party observes. Although some meteor tracks will be observed even from a suburban location, you'll have the best luck if your observing site is a good distance from city lights. You will need to prepare a finder chart and distribute copies to every observing-team member. This should be done well in advance of your observing party.

ACTIVITY 2-1

Preparing Finder Charts for a Meteor Shower

Let's assume that you intend to observe the Perseid meteor shower during mid-August. The meteoroids producing this shower originate from a point in the constellation Perseus (the *radiant*) and come from the tail of Comet Swift-Tuttle. (A *constellation* is a convenient star pattern.)

You can observe the Perseids from July 17 to August 24, with the most meteor tracks per hour (up to 160 per hour) observed on or near August 12. The actual number of meteor tracks you observe will vary with the year and your location.

Looking up Perseus on your planisphere for August 12, you learn that the constellation rises above the north-northeastern horizon at about 8:00 P.M. Since observing very close to the horizon is difficult, you'll advance your planisphere to 11:00 P.M. and plan observations for 11:00 P.M. to midnight.

Figure 2-1. *Finder chart for Perseid meteor shower, August 12 at around 11:00 P.M.*

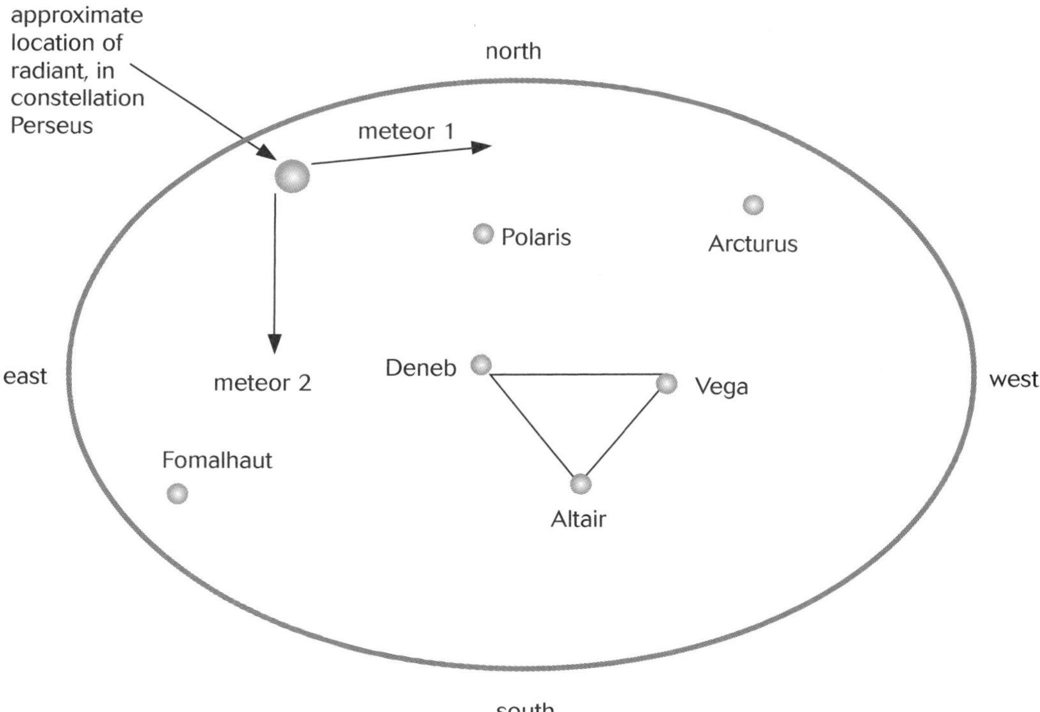

Star Key
Polaris—the North star, brightest star in constellation Ursa Minor
Fomalhaut—brightest star in constellation Pisces Australis
Deneb—brightest star in constellation Cygnus
Altair—brightest star in constellation Aquila
Vega—brightest star in constellation Lyra
Acturus—brightest star in constellation Bootes
Altair, Vega, and Deneb comprise the "Summer Triangle"

To prepare a finder chart for this date and time, copy onto a piece of paper the necessary information from your planisphere. Your finder chart should include the cardinal points of the compass and the positions of the brightest stars. The expected radiant of the meteor shower should also be marked on your finder chart to help with drawing observed meteor trails. Figure 2-1 presents a simple finder chart prepared for the Perseid meteor shower on August 12 at around 11:00 P.M. Note that two sample meteor tracks have been included.

You can hold this finder chart over your head and use it as you would your planisphere to orient yourself in the sky using the bright stars as celestial landmarks.

ACTIVITY 2-2

Meteor-Observing Party

All your friends should review your finder chart and acquaint themselves with the bright stellar "landmarks" of the night sky before you begin to observe meteors.

If you are working with a large number of meteor observers, it's a good idea to keep a master finder chart onto which everyone's individual observations can later be transferred. You might wish to delegate tasks—Harriet might keep track of the time and announce it to all observers at five-minute intervals, John might observe the northern sky, and Shari might record John's observations. To avoid duplication, have different team members concentrate on different sky quadrants. If you have four observers, for instance, one should look north from the radiant, one east, one west, and one south. Each time a meteor track is sighted, the observer should announce this observation and the data should be recorded by the delegated team member. You're now ready to begin observing meteor tracks. Good hunting!

The number of meteor tracks observed per hour is not the only significant information that can be obtained by your observing party. You could also trace out observed meteor tracks on the finder charts to get an idea of the angular length in degrees of a meteor's visible track. This can be used to estimate the true track length in kilometers.

ACTIVITY 2-3

Estimating Meteor Track Length

If a meteor track goes from one horizon through the *zenith* (the point in the sky directly over your head) to the other horizon, it traverses an angle of 180°. If it extends from the horizon to the zenith, it traverses 90°. Likewise, if it goes from a near-horizon radiant halfway to the zenith, it traverses 45°of arc.

Meteor track lengths can be calculated from meteor height above the surface of the Earth and the track angular extent, as shown in Figure 2-2. Let's say that you have determined that a meteor's path traverses an angle of a degrees from the fraction of the sky that it covers. (If it traverses half the sky, $a = 90°$. If it traverses one-quarter of the sky, $a = 45°$.) If the height of the meteor above the surface is h kilometers, the approximate length of the meteor's track (l, kilometers) can be shown to be:

$$l = ah/60$$

This simple equation is a good approximation if the meteor traverses an angular path of less than about 30°. More complex formulas can be used in the case of angular paths of larger meteor tracks.

Remember from our previous discussion that the height of a meteor track is 100 to 150 km above the surface of Earth. Let's say that we have observed a meteor track with an angular extent of 30° of arc. Using this formula, the approximate length of this track will be (100 × 30)/60 to (150 × 30)/60, or from 50 to 75 km. Now try repeating this calculation to estimate the lengths of meteor tracks that you observe.

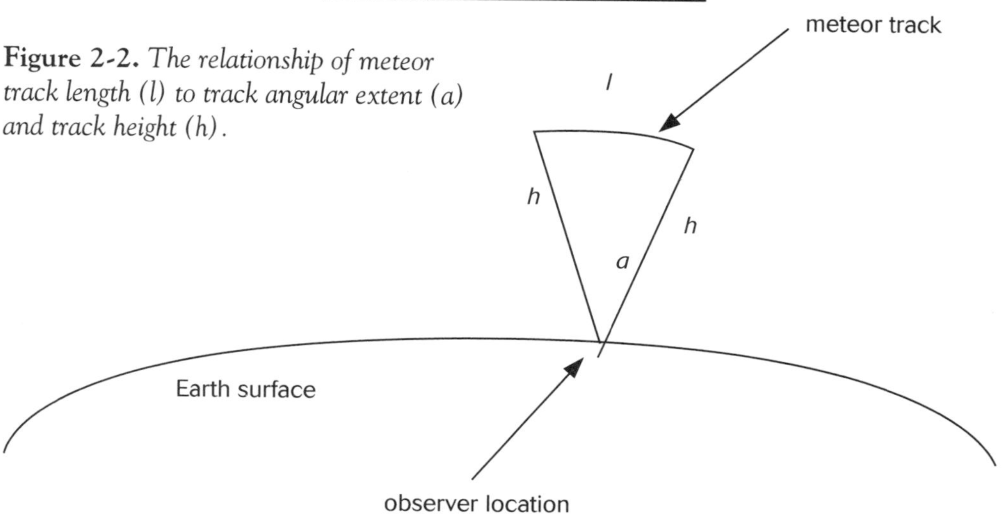

Figure 2-2. *The relationship of meteor track length (l) to track angular extent (a) and track height (h).*

Meteors, Meteorites, and Life

Before the 1980s, most astronomers would have suspected little interaction between these small denizens of the solar system and terrestrial life. Expert opinion has almost entirely turned around.

Without meteorite impacts on the early Earth, our planet's oceans and atmosphere may never have formed. Large meteorites in more recent eras, such as the one that doomed the dinosaurs, are responsible for vast terrestrial climate changes as well the extinction of many species of life.

Recent evidence indicates that some forms of life might migrate between solar-system objects as a result of meteoroid impacts. Life could have evolved on Mars and Europa (a moon of Jupiter), as well on Earth. A large object hitting one of these low-gravity worlds could blow some of these life-forms into space. Because some primitive and evolved bacterial life-forms can survive for a long time in interplanetary space, it is not impossible that some of these organisms have reached the Earth.

One goal for the space-faring civilization of the twenty-first century will be to accurately chart the solar orbits of those comets and asteroids that might ultimately threaten the Earth, and develop methods of diverting threatening objects. High-flying aircraft and balloons are used to collect samples of fresh meteoritic dust in the atmosphere and return this material for analysis. As planning for these missions continues, research astronomers will continue to depend upon amateurs for their careful observations of meteor showers and sporadic bolides.

★3★
The Moon

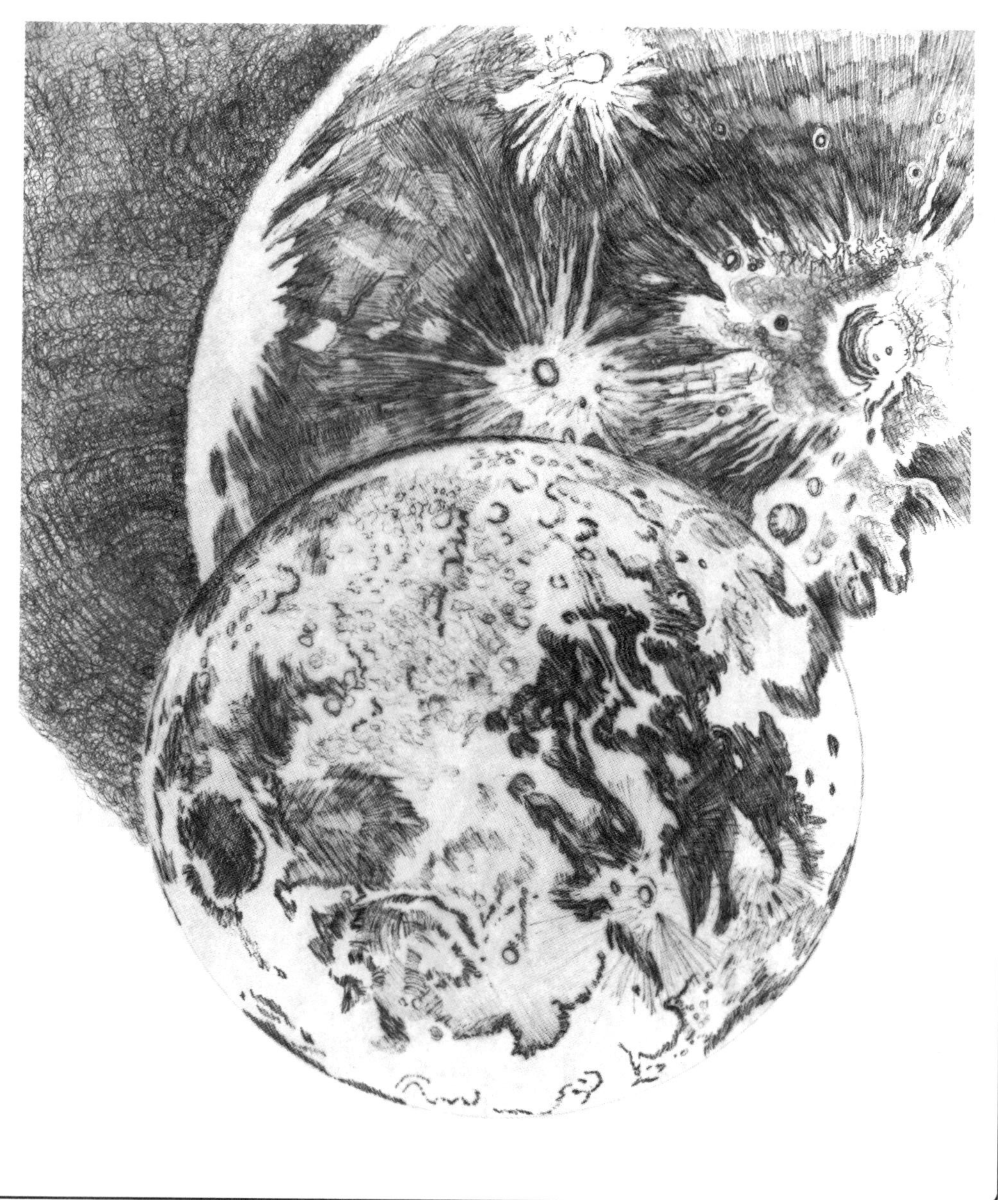

You may become an expert on meteors, and spend hours viewing planets, comets, and stars. But if your experience is like that of most who've viewed the universe through a telescope, your first and greatest love will be our planet's one natural satellite, the Moon.

The Moon in Myth and Legend

Perhaps it was in the New Stone Age or Neolithic era, when humans developed agriculture and built the first cities, that people first developed the idea that gods and goddesses ruled Earth, the Moon, the Sun, and the sky. Perhaps 10,000 years ago in the Neolithic Mediterranean cultures, the Moon became associated with female deities such as Diana, the Roman goddess of the Moon and the hunt.

It was important for early civilized humans to keep track of the motions of their celestial deities. So during the Bronze Age, when technology had improved to allow the moving and shaping of large stones, people began to erect stone circles to observe significant rising and setting points of the Moon and the Sun.

The most famous of the stone circles, and the best preserved, is Stonehenge in England. The earliest version of this monument was erected in the same era as the first Egyptian pyramids, about 5,000 years ago. According to modern computer simulations, an astronomer-priest could have stood at the center of a stone circle and sighted between stones at the Moon or the Sun near the horizon. He or she also could have kept track of eclipse cycles by moving markers in chalk-filled holes arranged around the circumference of Stonehenge.

The Aztecs (200 B.C.–A.D. 1500) and other civilized people of pre-Columbian Central and South America, observed the Moon from platforms atop pyramids. The Aztec goddess Coyolxauhqui was associated with the Moon. At certain times of month, Coyolxauhqui intrudes upon the domain of Mother Earth; at other times her brightness dims the stars, which represent the sky god.

The ancient Egyptians of North Africa associated the Moon with Osiris, a god who judged the dead and controlled the transformation from life to death. Osiris was also responsible for civilizing humans and bringing them law.

In one charming myth of the ancient Sumerians, who lived in what is now southern Iraq, the Moon god Nanna bestowed many gifts upon his sweetheart, the goddess Ningal. These gifts included the spring floods of the Tigris and Euphrates Rivers, the reeds of the marsh, agricultural bounty, and the dairy products of the herds.

Since the Moon is renewed each month, it has also become associated with immortality. This was especially true for the ancient Chinese Moon goddess Heng O, who had the power to dispense immortality. Perhaps in remembrance of Heng O, the Chinese recognize a "Lady in the Moon."

Modern astronomers are not alone in their admiration of the Moon. During the Old Stone Age, or Paleolithic era, when people were hunting mammoths and creating cave art, at least one person was systematically observing the phases of the Moon. More than 20,000 years ago, this person carefully engraved a record of lunar phases on an animal bone.

Physical Characteristics and Motions of the Moon

The Moon's mass is 73,700,000,000,000,000,000,000 kg, or one eighty-first that of the Earth. The average distance of the Moon from the Earth in its slightly elliptical orbit is a little less than 400,000 km. The Moon's diameter is about 3,500 km, about one-quarter that of the Earth. The average angular size of the Moon is about 0.5°, the same as that of the Sun.

ACTIVITY 3-1

Observing the Eccentricity of the Moon's Orbit

Because the Moon's orbit is slightly elliptical, it will appear a bit larger at closest approach to the Earth (perigee) than at greatest distance (apogee). A full Moon will not always occur at the same Earth-Moon separation. If you have a reticle eyepiece (see Appendix B for information on using a reticle eyepiece), you can observe variations in apparent lunar size from one full Moon to the next. You do this by observing the full Moon and sketching its appearance as seen through the eyepiece, including the eyepiece calibrations, at intervals of one month.

Over the billions of years that the Moon has orbited the Earth, *tides* (variation's in atmospheric levels) on the Moon produced by Earth's gravity have slowed the Moon's rotation. Today, the Moon rotates once every month, the same time that it takes to orbit the Earth. This is why we only see one hemisphere of the Moon from the Earth's surface. Robot probes and astronauts who have orbited the Moon have revealed the Moon's hidden hemisphere, or "far side."

The Moon's Phases

The orientation of the Moon in the major lunar *phases* (changes in apparent shape) is shown in Figure 3-1. The phase cycle results from the Moon's constantly changing position relative to the Earth and the Sun.

The lunar phase cycle begins with the new Moon. Because the Sun's rays only illuminate the Moon's far side, the Moon is invisible during this phase. The new Moon rises at (terrestrial) sunrise and sets at sunset.

A few days after new Moon, a small portion of the Moon becomes visible as a waxing crescent. The Moon in this phase rises in the morning and sets in the evening, With a good view of the western horizon, you can easily observe the waxing crescent Moon low in the western sky at sunset.

The first quarter Moon is often called the "half Moon" because one-half of the moon's visible face is illuminated. The Moon in this phase rises at noon and sets at midnight. The first quarter Moon is high in the sky at sunset and is therefore an easy observation target.

Figure 3-1. *The lunar phases.*

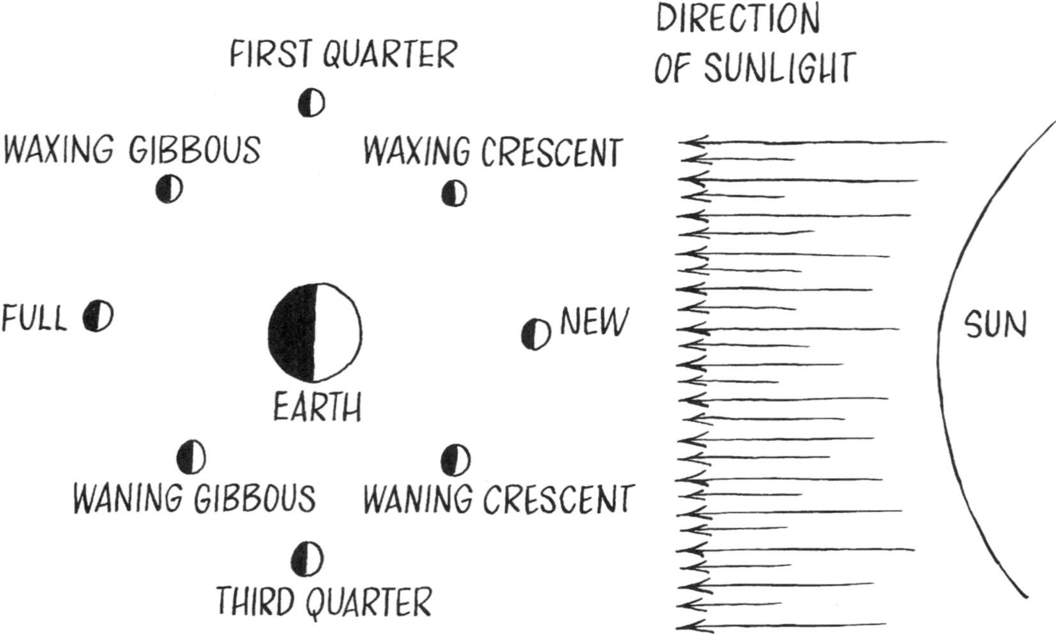

As the Moon *waxes* (increases in brighteness) toward full, it next passes through the waxing gibbous phase, in which it is three-quarters illuminated. The waxing gibbous Moon rises in the afternoon and sets in the predawn hours. The Moon in this phase is high in the sky during early evening observing sessions.

Since the full Moon rises at sundown and sets at sunrise, this phase is highest in the sky at midnight. In the early evening, the full Moon is easily observable in the eastern sky.

As the Moon begins to *wane* (decrease in brightness), it passes next through the waning gibbous phase, rising in the evening and seting in the morning. If you stay up late, you can observe this phase in the eastern sky around midnight.

During the third quarter, the Moon is once again half illuminated. But the half of the Moon visible during this phase is the half that was invisible during the first quarter. The third quarter Moon rises at midnight and sets at noon. You'll see it low in the east in the predawn sky.

The final lunar phase is the waning crescent. The Moon rises in the predawn hours and sets in early afternoon, and is consequently not a convenient observation target.

Since the Earth *revolves* (orbits) around the Sun while the Moon revolves around the Earth, the Moon rises above the eastern horizon about 50 minutes later each day. From the viewpoint of a terrestrial observer, the lunar phase cycle repeats once every 29.5 days, which is defined as a lunar month.

ACTIVITY 3-2
Keeping Track of Lunar and Solar Motions

Since the Earth revolves around the Sun as the Moon revolves around the Earth, the Moon's position in the sky will change from one full Moon to the next. You can observe this by looking at the full Moon and the star field near it through a low-power eyepiece at monthly intervals. You may wish to experiment with color filters to reduce the glare of the full Moon. Use a pencil and paper to sketch your view of the Moon and the stars around it.

Moon Features

When you observe the Moon, remember that the lunar image in your telescope eyepiece is inverted (see Figures 3-2A and B). As your observations will reveal, there are three basic terrain types on the Moon's visible face. These are maria, highlands, and craters.

Figure 3-2A. *The first quarter Moon.*

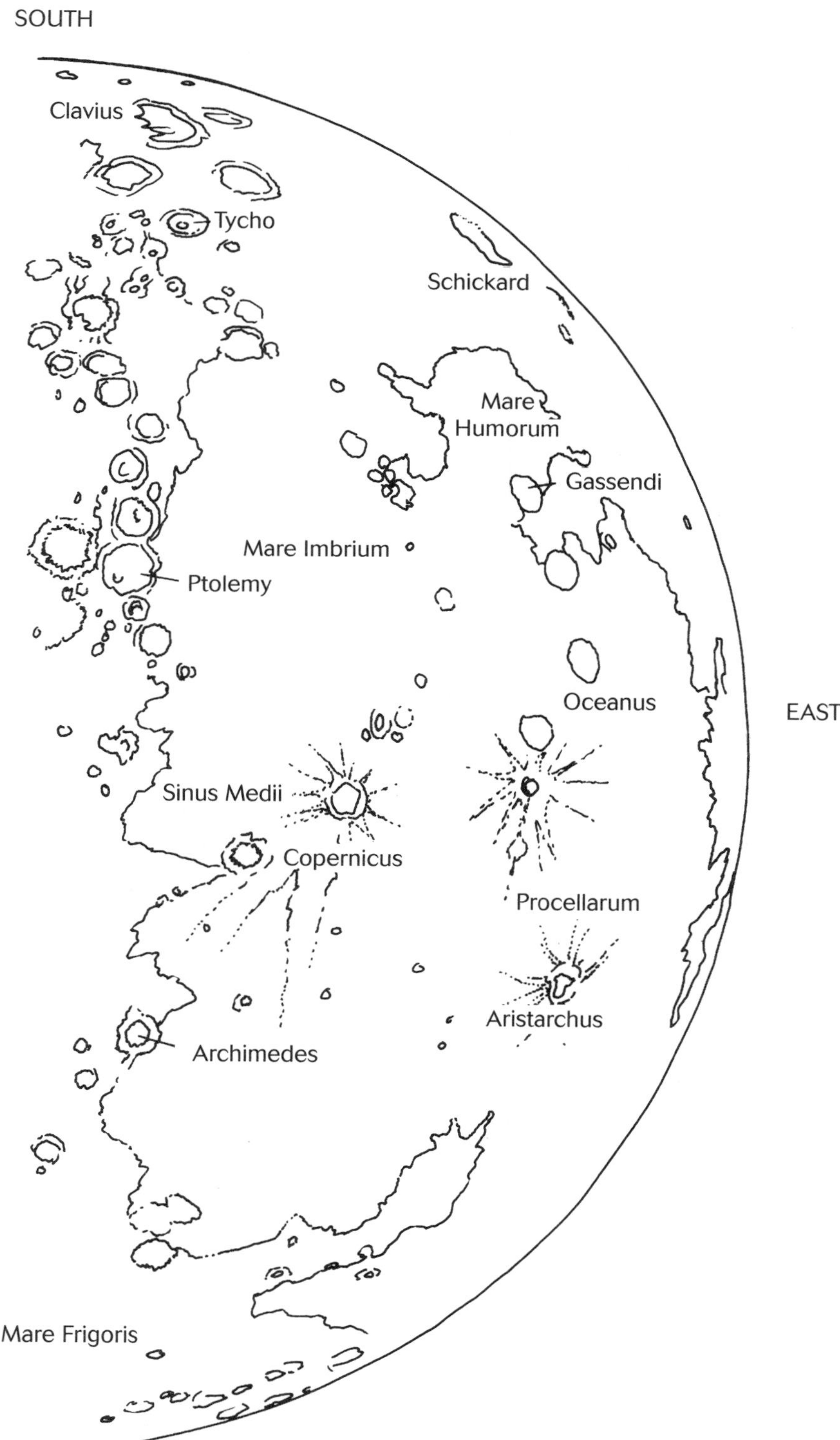

Figure 3-2B. *The third quarter Moon.*

The *maria* (singular *mare*) are large, relatively flat regions that are hundreds of kilometers across and are darker than the surrounding terrain. Although originally thought to be watery seas (*maria* means "seas"), the totally dry maria probably formed as a result of impacts by large meteoroids.

The lighter highlands contain mountain ranges and ridges. Some of the lunar peaks approximate Mount Everest in height.

Through a low-power eyepiece (such as 35×), you can observe many lunar craters in both maria and highlands. All or most of these craters formed when large and small meteroids hit the Moon during our satellite's 4.5 billion–year history. Around some of these craters, you will see rays that formed when ejected material fell back toward the surface. Others have crater walls or central peaks. Cental peaks in lunar craters may have been formed when lunar material ejected by an impact rebounded. Crater walls are built-up deposits of ejected material pushed from the impact center by the force of the impact.

ACTIVITY 3-3

Simulating Crater Formation

You can experiment with impact events on celestial objects using very low-tech tools. Take a tray and fill it with mud. If you drop pebbles on the mud, you'll be able to observe the craters resulting from the impact. Try directing the pebbles obliquely (from the side) instead of vertically to see if you can produce an odd-shaped crater or ejecta stream similiar to a lunar crater's rays.

ACTIVITY 3-4

The Rays of Copernicus

You will easily find this rayed crater near the center of the third quarter Moon, or east of center of the full Moon. Experiment with color filters to improve the contrast of the rays against the surrounding terrain. Then use a pencil and paper to sketch the rays. Do you see a different concentration of rays on one side of the crater than on the other? What direction do you think the meteroid that produced the crater came from?

As lunar phases change, even a casual observer will notice how the shadows of various lunar features vary with phase. It's fun to keep track of these variations. You may find, in fact, that your most rewarding lunar observations take place when the Moon is less than full. This is because shadows cast by various features are longer at nonfull phases, increasing the visual contrast, as shown in Figure 3-3.

Figure 3-3. *Long shadows on the lunar surface.*

ACTIVITY 3-5

The Central Peak of Tycho

During the waxing gibbous Moon and after, you will notice the great crater Tycho near the Moon's south pole. The walls of this crater are 4 km high, and Tycho's diameter is approximately 80 km. The many chains of craterlets that extend outward from Tycho make this one of the most prominent rayed craters on the Moon's surface.

Try observing the shadow cast by the central peak of Tycho. Can you see how this shadow changes with lunar phase?

ACTIVITY 3-6

The Mountains near Schickard

Near the Moon's southeast edge is a crater called Schickard which is about 200 km in diameter. After full Moon, the *terminator* (boundary between light and dark) will move toward this feature. You can observe the shadows cast by mountains in the vicinity of Schickard. At what lunar phase are these shadows most visible?

As mentioned earlier, you may wish to experiment with color filters that screw onto your telescope's eyepiece to reduce the glare of the full Moon and relieve eyestrain. But there is an alternative approach to reducing lunar glare.

ACTIVITY 3-7

Masking Your Telescope's Aperture

Another way to reduce lunar glare is to reduce your telescope's light-gathering power (LGP). One way of doing this has been described by Philip S. Harrington (*Star Ware*, Wiley, 1994). Cut a piece of cardboard that will cover the aperture of your telescope. Make a central hole in the cardboard that is smaller than the telescope's aperture and tape the cardboard to your telescope. In this way, less moonlight will get in and glare will be reduced. If the cardboard reduces the aperture of your telescope by 50 percent, the Moon's brightness will be reduced by up to one-fourth of its unmasked value. *CAUTION: To avoid eye damage, never try this to observe the Sun.*

Eclipses of the Moon and the Sun

By a happy coincidence, the Moon and the Sun are about the same angular size when viewed from the Earth. That means that when the Moon is aligned between the Sun and the Earth during the new Moon, the Moon blocks the Sun's light and we view a solar *eclipse* (see Figure 3-4). When these three celes-

Figure 3-4. *A solar eclipse. (Note: Earth, Moon, and Sun are not to scale.)*

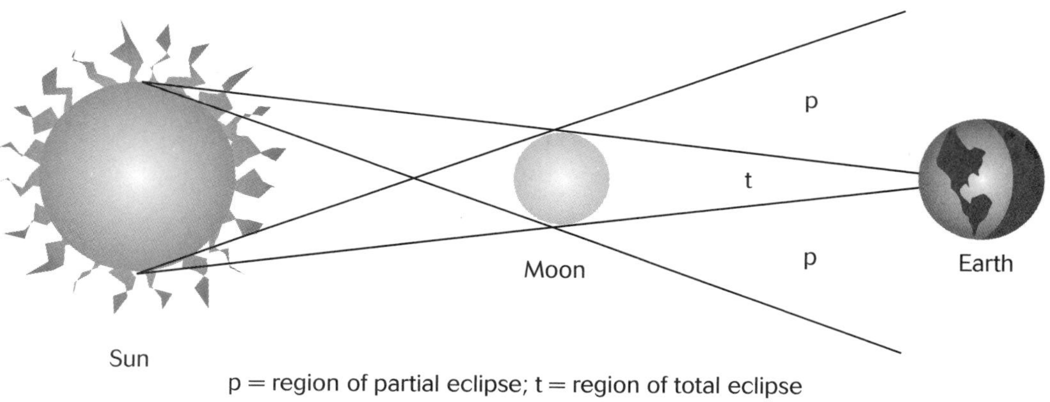

tial objects align so that the Earth is between the Sun and the Moon during the full Moon phase, we experience a lunar eclipse as the Earth's shadow falls on the Moon (see Figure 3-5). The Moon's path in the sky does not coincide with the Sun's path, which is called the *ecliptic*. Eclipses can occur only when the Moon's path and the ecliptic cross at new or full Moon.

Note the way light rays from the Sun pass by the Moon's edge (or limb) in Figure 3-4. This shows why a *total eclipse*, when the solar disk is entirely obscured by the Moon, is seen only from places on Earth where the central region of the Moon's shadow is projected. Places on Earth in the outer regions of the Moon's shadow will experience a *partial eclipse*, in which only a part of the Sun's disk is obscured.

If a solar eclipse occurs when the moon is near apogee, a ring of sunlight will be visible around the solar portion obscured by the Moon. This is called an *annular eclipse*.

Figure 3-5. *A lunar eclipse. (Note: Earth, Moon, and Sun are not to scale.)*

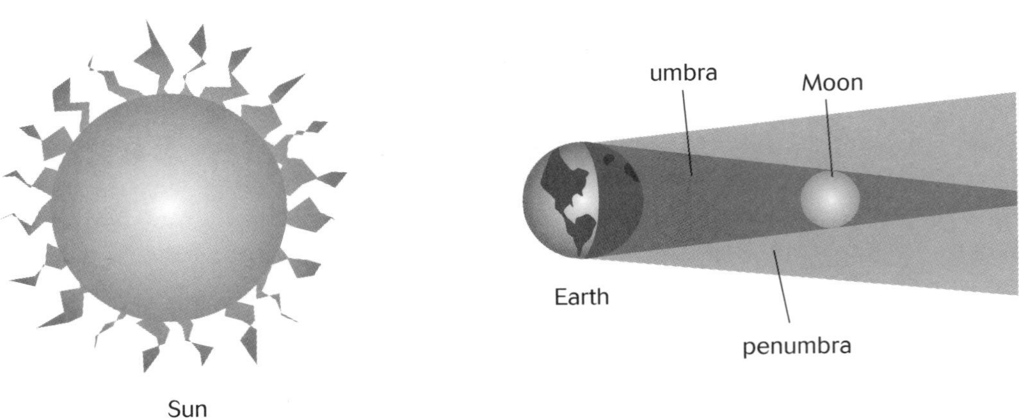

The full Moon is usually visible during a lunar eclipse, but its color is changed because all light reachiing it has been refracted through Earth's atmosphere. As discussed in my earlier book, *Telescope Power* (Wiley, 1993), you can observe lunar color changes during lunar eclipses. Atmospheric dust or pollution results in the darkest eclipses. A schedule of solar and lunar eclipses is given in Appendix C.

Lunar Occultations

To an observer on the Earth, the Moon is the largest object in the night sky. It is also closer to the Earth than other large celestial objects. Sometimes, as the Moon moves through the night sky, it passes in front of, or *occults*, a bright star or planet. The predicted times for such occultations are usually announced well in advance in monthly astronomical publications such as *Astronomy* and *Sky & Telescope*.

Occultation events are very significant to a number of astronomical disciplines. Imagine that you wish to observe a double-star pair that consists of a bright and a dim star. The dim star may be much easier to study when the light of its brighter companion is temporarily occulted.

ACTIVITY 3-8

Observing Lunar Occultations

If you view an occultation event, you may wish to see how the predicted times for star/planet disappearance or reappearance agree with your observations. Irregularities in the lunar surface are one reason for such discrepancies. If a lunar mountain occults a star or planet, the occultation will be somewhat early. It will be late if the occulting portion of the Moon is a depressed region such as a crater. Timing lunar occultations can reveal details about lunar topography.

The Moon and Earth's Tides

One great triumph of Newtonian physics was the understanding of how the Moon (and to a lesser extent, the Sun) produces tides in terrestrial oceans. As shown in Figure 3-6, the portion of Earth's oceans that is closest to the Moon is the portion most attracted to the Moon. A high tide therefore exists in this area.

Figure 3-6. *The effect of the Moon on Earth's tides. (Note: Earth and Moon are not to scale.)*

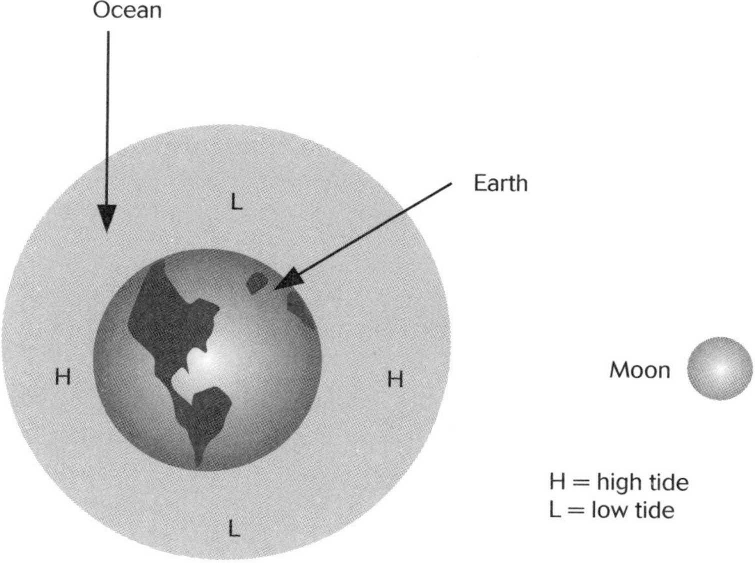

The portion of the ocean on the side of Earth opposite this point is less attracted by the Moon than nearby water is. Water tends to build up here as a second high tide. At the intermediate locations shown, there is a low tide. There are two high tides and two low tides each day.

This picture is greatly simplified because no provision is made for the effects of land or the Sun's attraction, which complicates the tidal picture. The greatest range between high and low tides occurs at full and new Moons, when the Moon and the Sun pull in approximately the same direction.

As well as oceanic tides, the Moon and the Sun produce tidal variations in Earth's atmosphere. At high tide, the Earth's atmosphere extends a little farther above the surface than at low tide.

ACTIVITY 3-9

Observing the Moon's Effect on the Tides

If you live near or visit a beach, you can observe the tidal range by keeping track of the location of the water's edge. Does high tide occur when the Moon is directly overhead? Are high tides higher and low tides lower at your location when the Moon is full?

The Astronaut's Moon

One of the most memorable accomplishments of the twentieth century was the series of Moon landings by American astronauts as part of Project Apollo. During the late 1960s and early 1970s, nine Apollo craft carrying three men each orbited or flew by the Moon. Lunar modules carrying two men each separated from the main craft and landed on the Moon during the flights of *Apollo 11*, *12*, *14*, *15*, *16*, and *17*.

One result of these explorations was a fresh appreciation of the Earth as a life-bearing world. Another was an understanding of the Moon's nature and origin.

We now know that our Moon is a geologically dead world without the crustal movements, volcanism, and earthquakes that characterize our home planet's dynamic geology. The Moon has no magnetic field to speak of and no atmosphere. Without an atmosphere or magnetic field to protect it, the Moon's surface is constantly bombarded by *solar wind* (a stream of electrically charged particles emitted by the Sun) and the more energetic *cosmic rays* (high-energy electrically charged particles accelerated by celestial magnetic fields), which originate in our galaxy or beyond.

Rocks collected during Apollo expeditions reveal a great deal about the origin of the Earth-Moon system. Scientists used to believe that the Moon was formed in place at the same time as the Earth during the formation of the solar system, or that it was captured by our planet from an independent solar orbit. But the actual rock samples showed that the oldest rocks on the Earth and the Moon are almost exactly the same age, which does not support the theory of an independent lunar origin. Since the oldest rocks on both the Earth and the Moon are younger than the solar system, the Earth and the Moon probably did not begin in place.

Most scientists now adhere to another scenario. They imagine that in the early days of the solar system, Earth coalesced (came together) alone without a natural satellite. Then a little more than four billion years ago, it was struck by a wandering planet or giant comet close to the size of present-day Mars. The Earth was heated to the molten state by this enormous impact and much material was ejected into space. Some of this material later coalesced as our Moon.

★4★ Comets

Before the age of science, these celestial marvels were a fearful sight. People consulted soothsayers and priests, hid in caves, and quaked in terror at their passage. Today we understand comets and proudly show them off to friends when they appear in our telescope eyepiece. And we often forget that human fear of these unpredictible "hairy stars" actually influenced the course of human history.

Comets in Myth and History

Something like 100,000 cometary *apparitions* (visits to the inner solar system) have been observed in the million or so years that humans have watched the skies. Almost all cultures have considered comets to be portents of evil. According to the Masai in Africa, the appearance of a comet in the sky was an omen of famine; the Zulus believed that comets brought war; other African peoples blamed comets for disease and the death of a ruler.

In the Middle Bronze Age, around 3,500 years ago, a Chinese ruler named Chieh unjustly executed his counselors. Retribution for this high-level crime was paid by the appearance of a comet in the sky. A few hundred years later, another comet was visible in China during a war between two provinces. Military disaster was predicted for one faction because the comet's tail pointed in their direction.

While comets foretold disaster, there was widespread disagreement about what could be done, if anything, to overcome the omen. Some believed in the power of prayer; others such as some Chinese scholars of about 500 B.C., considered a comet a heavenly broom, intent on sweeping away evil. For evildoers, prayer would be of no avail when a comet was in the sky.

Because of their fascination with these fearful heavenly visitors, the Chinese began early in their history the systematic observation of cometary apparitions. Between 1400 B.C. and A.D. 100, they observed and recorded at least 338 separate apparitions, including such details as the length and number of tails.

Other ancient people, notably the Babylonians and the Egyptians, systematically observed cometary apparitions. There is some evidence that they attempted to correlate disasters such as floods and earthquakes with cometary apparitions.

Ancient Greeks and Romans continued the tradition of comet observation and interpretation. Some Greek scholars guessed correctly and considered comets to be members of the solar system. Unfortunately, Aristotle (384–322 B.C.), one of the most influential of Greek philosophers, erred in his conclusion that comets were a meteorological rather than a celestial phenomenon.

Perhaps the most historically significant cometary apparition was the appearance of Halley's comet over Europe in 1066. An army from northern France led by the Norman king William was bogged down near their invasion beaches in England as they faced the seasoned troops of Harold, the Saxon king. The bright apparition of Comet Halley drove the superstitious soldiers of both armies to despair. William won the Battle of Hastings, conquered England—and became known as William the Conqueror—in part because he convinced his soldiers that the comet was a bad omen for the Saxons.

THE MOST FAMOUS COMET

Comet Halley, the most famous comet in the solar system, returns to the inner solar system at intervals of about 76 years. It is named after the seventeenth-century British astronomer Edmund Halley (1656–1742), who applied Newton's theory of gravity to demonstrate that this comet was periodic and to predict its next appearance. Many apparitions of this comet were recorded by ancient Chinese observers.

Visual Aspects of Comets

Comets are dramatic to the naked eye because some of them rival the brightest stars in the sky. But a great deal more detail will be revealed by your telescope, even under low power. On average, a bright comet appears in our skies once every few years. These cometary apparitions are usually covered in local newspapers as well as monthly astronomy publications.

To observe a comet, you'll need a site as removed as possible from bright city streetlights. If you live in an urban location, you might try a city park or beach. (Be sure an adult goes with you on your comet-watching expedition.)

Since a comet is a large object, use a low-power eyepiece (such as 35×). Try sketching the visual appearance of the comet as viewed through your telescope. If your telescope is equipped with an electrical clock drive and is properly aligned with geographic north, the comet will remain in the eyepiece's field of view for hours. But even without a clock drive, the comet will be visible in your low-power telescope without realignment for at least a few minutes.

Cometary orbits are very elliptical. Those of long-period comets can extend trillions of kilometers when farthest from the Sun. Such comets take as long as 100,000 years to complete one orbit. Short-period comets can approach the Sun within 100,000,000 km, but spend much of their decades-long orbits 1,000,000,000 km or farther from the Sun.

Figure 4-1 shows the structure of a typical comet when it is far from the Sun and during an apparition. Far from the Sun, the comet consists of a nucleus of

Figure 4-1. *Features of a typical comet, far from the Sun (top) and during a close solar approach (bottom).*

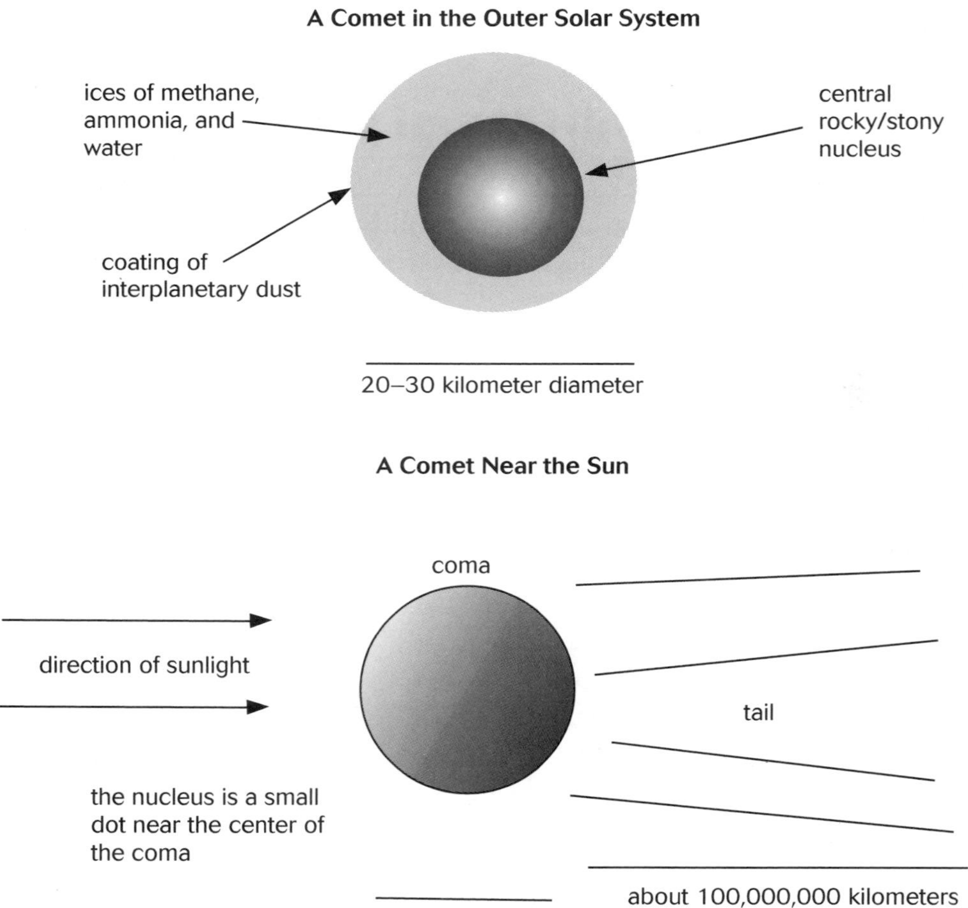

rock and stone surrounded by layers of frozen methane, ammonia, and water. These ices in some comets have a layer of dust around them. The diameter of a typical comet in the outer reaches of the solar system is 20 to 30 km. Far from the Sun, a comet is a very dim object only visible through large telescopes.

As the comet moves sunward in its elliptical orbit, a number of changes in its appearance take place. Heat from the Sun vaporizes some of the ice, and the nucleus becomes enveloped in a roughly spherical gas cloud called the *coma*. The coma's diameter may be tens of thousands of kilometers. It is this feature that makes the comet appear to the unassisted eye and under telescopic magnification as a fuzzy star.

ACTIVITY 4-2

Estimating the Size of a Comet's Coma

If your telescope is equipped with a low-magnification reticle eyepiece, you can use this device to estimate the angular size of a comet's coma. You may wish first to calibrate the reticle eyepiece using the full Moon, which has an angular extent of about 0.5°. (See Appendix B for information on using a reticle eyepiece.)

If the comet is a distance of d kilometers from the Earth and it extends an approximate angle of a degrees of arc, the approximate diameter of the coma, c, in kilometers, is

$$c = da/60$$

Let's say that the newspapers have reported that the comet is at an approximate distance of 10,000,000 km on the night you observe it. If the coma is half the size of the full Moon, then $a = 0.25°$ and the coma's approximate diameter is 42,000 km.

In addition to heating the comet, *photons* (the smallest individual units of electromagnetic energy) of sunlight are capable of pushing against the evaporated gas and dust. (This phenomenon is called *radiation pressure*.) This material trails from the comet's coma in the direction opposite the Sun and looks like a tail. The tail's length may be 100,000,000 km or longer, but it is so tenuous that you could pack all tail material into a suitcase. Typical comets have enough ice to produce tails on dozens or more visits to the inner solar system.

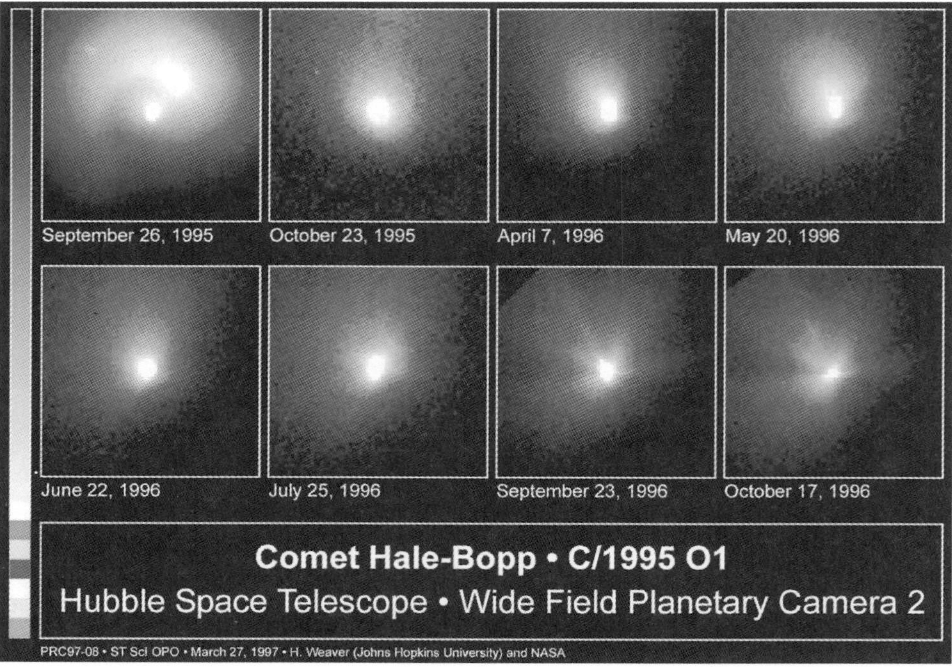

Figure 4-2. *Comet Hale-Bopp as seen from the Hubble Space Telescope.*

ACTIVITY 4-3

Keeping Track of a Comet's Progress

Comets move rapidly during their close solar pass. You can keep track of a comet's progress by sketching the coma and surrounding star field on consecutive nights. If you then identify the stars you have sketched using a finder chart, you can plot the progress of the coma's center, which is the approximate location of the nucleus.

Astronomers use observations of a comet's motion across the star field to estimate the comet's velocity relative to the Earth. To do this, they must also know the approximate distance of the comet from the Earth.

Let's say a comet is observed to shift position by s degrees per day when it is d kilometers from the Earth. The comet's velocity in kilometers per day relative to the Earth is approximately equal to $sd/60$. To convert this velocity to approximate kilometers per second, divide by 100,000.

Because dust grains and vaporized ice react differently to the pressure of sunlight, there may be two tails—one of dust and one of gas. Both comet tails point away from the Sun.

Observatories above the Earth's atmosphere have been used to study comets in wavelengths of light other than the visible. We know that various types of chemical reactions may occur in the heated gas as the comet proceeds sunward. Many comets have a hydrogen cloud 1,000,000 km in diameter surrounding the coma.

ACTIVITY 4-4

Observing Changes in a Comet's Tail

The ancients were fascinated (and frightened) by the changes in a comet's tail. Try sketching the appearance of a comet's tail on successive nights. How many tails are there? Does their appearance change with time?

Where Do Comets Come From?

Astronomers know of two distinct comet populations. Short-period comets visit the inner solar system at intervals of about a century or less frequently. Their farthest distance from the Sun is typically 30 to 50 *astronomical units* (AU). One astronomical unit is the average Earth-Sun separation (about 150,000,000 km).

In recent years, astronomers have made progress in their understanding of the origin of short-period comets. There is a region in the solar system between about 30 and 50 AU from the Sun called the *Kuiper belt*. This region is inhabited by thousands of large and small icy bodies. The largest Kuiper belt object (KBO) is the planet Pluto, which has a diameter of about 3,000 km and a mass about 20 percent of the Moon's.

There may be as many as 100,000 Kuiper belt *cometoids*, which range from a few kilometers to 1,000 km in radius. The gravitational attraction of the giant planets Jupiter, Saturn, Uranus, and Neptune occasionally pull these small bodies toward the inner solar system. Those that are drawn into highly elliptical orbits, with *perihelia* (closest approaches to the sun) less than a few astronomical units from the Sun, will heat up and develop comas and tails during close solar approaches.

While it is possible to predict the appearance of a short-period or periodic comet in our sky, this is not the case for a long-period comet. Comets of this population have *aphelia* (farthest points from the Sun) up to 100,000 AU and perihelia within a few astronomical units. Long-period comets require 10,000 years or longer to complete one revolution of the Sun.

The source for these comets is the *Oort Cloud*. This spherical shell extends to about 100,000 AU (almost half the distance to our Sun's nearest stellar neighbor). As many as one trillion comets may inhabit the Oort Cloud; each measures 20 to 30 kilometers in diameter.

Long-period comets are directed sunward by the passage of other stars at intervals of about one million years through the outer fringes of the Oort Cloud. This is because the stars slowly shift position as they move around the center of our Milky Way Galaxy. (A *galaxy* is a grouping of billions of stars.) At rare intervals, stars may be a good deal closer to us than our nearest stellar neighbors today.

The discoveries of long-period comets are random events since their apparitions cannot be predicted. Because many long-period comets have made very few solar passes, they have a thicker layer of interplanetary dust than short-period comets. Therefore, long-period comets often put on a less dramatic sky show than their short-period counterparts.

ACTIVITY 4-5

Observing Stellar Occultations by Comets

Occasionally, a comet's coma may pass in front of and occult a bright *star* (a self-luminous celestial object). Such occultations are predicted in advance, when possible, in monthly publications such as *Sky & Telescope* and *Astronomy* magazines.

When observing a star's occultation by a comet, try to record the times of the event's beginning and end. If the bright star is still slightly visible through the comet's coma, try to estimate how much it is dimmed. Such observations can help astronomers estimate the amount of material in a comet's coma.

Some astronomers have suggested that neighboring stars may play a form of "tennis" and exchange comets back and forth. No clear evidence of a true interstellar comet has thus far been reported.

Comets and the Solar System's Evolution

Comets seem to be composed of the primordial "star stuff" out of which the solar system condensed. Five billion years ago, there was no Earth, Moon, planets, or Sun. Instead, there was a diffuse gas cloud, or *nebula*, trillions of kilometers across.

This nebula was mostly hydrogen and helium until gas streamed in from a nearby exploding star. During the supernova event that marks the demise of a star much more massive than the Sun, elements much more massive than helium are created and dispersed into space. (See Chapter 7 for information on supernovas.)

The turbulence created by the interacting gas caused the nebula to develop "clumps," or condensations. Large clumps became *protostars*—objects that would ultimately evolve into energy-generating stars. Smaller clumps became the *protoplanets*. These would eventually evolve into planetary systems that apparently attend most or all stars in the universe. (A *planet* is a celestial object orbiting a star and shining by reflected light.)

Not all the nebular material condensed into stars or planets. Some became cometary objects that crisscrossed the infant solar systems. Comets brought volatile materials such as water, carbon dioxide, and nitrogen to the newly formed inner planets of our solar system and others. As life developed on some of these star-warmed inner worlds, other comets occasionally impacted these worlds.

Do Comets Hit Earth?

A small comet fell in Siberia in 1908. This comet had a diameter of only a few hundred meters and the destructive force was equivalent to that of a large thermonuclear bomb, without the radiation. Fortunately, the impact occurred in a sparsely populated region and loss of life was minimal.

Large cometary bodies measuring kilometers in diameter impact the Earth much less frequently, at intervals of tens of millions of years. The meteroid that wiped out the dinosaurs about 65 million years ago may have been a comet.

Comet Exploration

The first exploration of a comet occured in 1986 during the most recent apparition of Comet Halley. A flotilla of robotic space probes from the United States, the USSR, Western Europe, and Japan flew through Halley's coma and tail and measured the comet's properties with many instruments. The European probe

Giotto performed the closest approach to the comet's nucleus and determined that the potato-shaped dark nucleus of a comet is one of the least reflective bodies in the solar system. Photographs revealed jets of ice and dust evaporating from the nucleus. Other instruments studied the composition of the comet's coma and tail. Further probes will undoubtedly reveal more details of the comet's nucleus.

Future robotic cometary explorers may use advanced electric-propulsion systems or solar sails to maneuver to a low-speed rendezvous with a comet near perihelion. These craft could fly in formation with the comet for weeks or months. Samples of cometary material could be returned to laboratories on Earth or in low Earth orbit by these probes.

ACTIVITY 4-6

Comet Viewing with Color Filters

Comets are complex, ever-changing sky creatures. As suggested by Philip S. Harrington in *Star Ware,* (Wiley, 1994), you can have a great deal of fun viewing these denizens of deep space through color filters. Which color gives the best views? Does the same color filter give best results on consecutive nights, or do comet colors alter as these objects approach or recede from perihelion? If comet color changes with distance from the Sun, what do you think causes this change?

★5★
The Sun

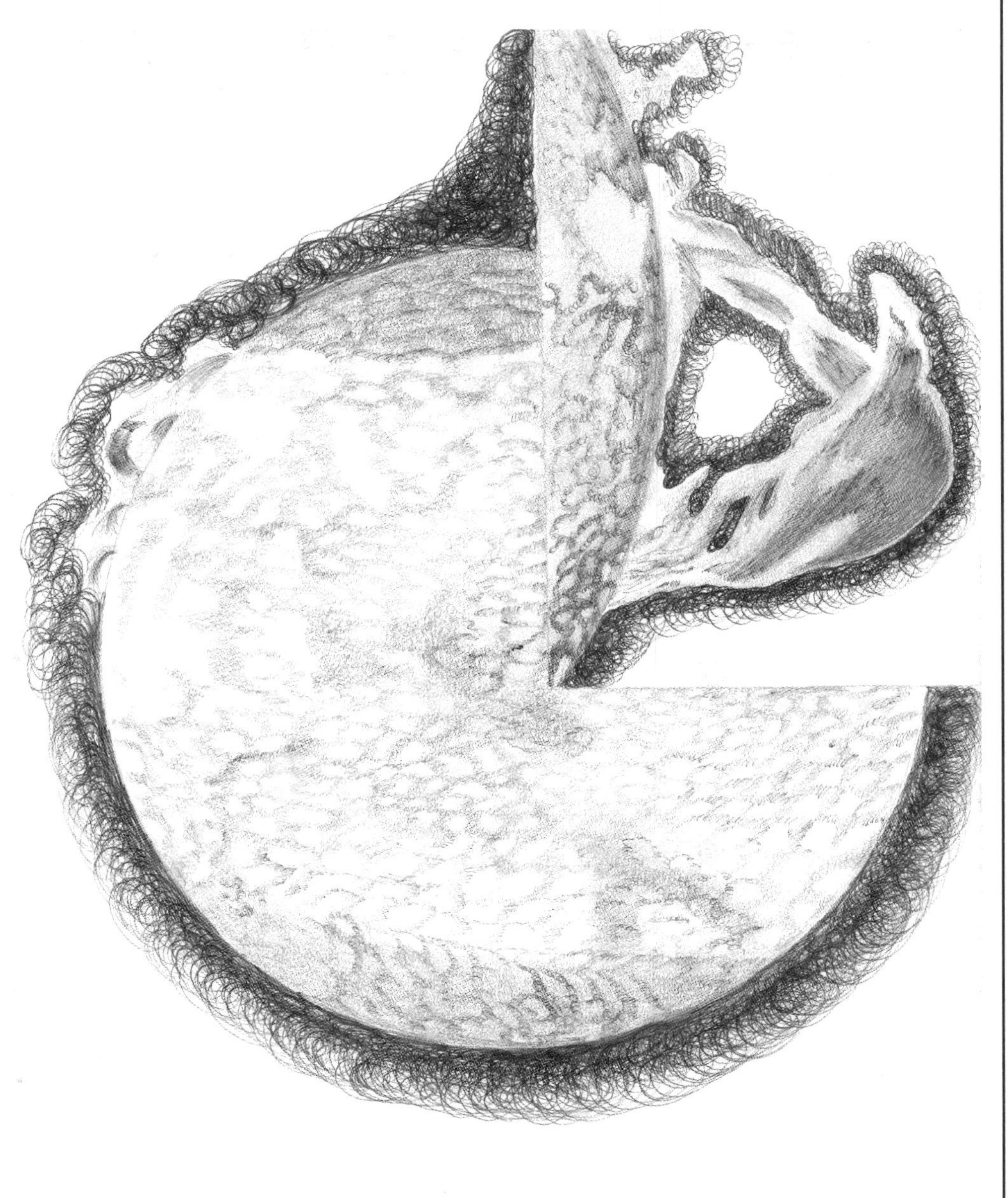

Our Sun is a pretty typical star, not much different from billions of other stars that inhabit the Milky Way Galaxy and galaxies beyond. But from the human point of view, it's crucial. Terrestrial life would simply be impossible were it not for the proximity of a star stable enough to support the conditions we've had on the Earth for billions of years.

The Sun is about halfway through its 10 billion–year life expectancy. But as it ages, it will expand and radiate more light. In perhaps two billion years, any remaining terrestrial life will be forced to emigrate from Earth or be engulfed in the hugely expanded Sun.

The Visible Sun

In considering our Sun, a good starting place is the basic difference between a star and a planet. Unlike a planet, which shines by reflected light, stars emit light that they create. Stars generate their energy by nuclear processes deep within their interior. Some very massive blue stars burn so rapidly that they exhaust their nuclear fuel store within a few million years. Low-mass red stars burn at a slower rate and may remain stable for 100 billion to a trillion years. Our Sun is between these two extremes.

Star Color, Mass, Surface Temperature, and Life Expectancy

Deep in their interiors, where matter is converted into energy, all stars are pretty much alike. The *thermonuclear fusion zone*, also called the *nuclear fusion zone*, is a region of multimillion-degree temperatures. A star's color, however, can tell us a great deal about stellar variation.

Low-mass stars may be 50 times or more massive than Jupiter, or one-twentieth the mass of the Sun. Such stars have surface temperatures of about 3,000°C. The low surface temperature reveals that the star's nuclear furnace is burning slowly. Some red stars may shine for 100 billion years or longer.

Yellow stars such as the Sun generate more energy and have hotter surfaces, with temperatures of about 6,000°C. Stars of approximate solar mass (about the same mass as the Sun) have life expectancies measured in billions of years.

The most energetic and hottest stars in the sky are blue. Some of these are 20 to 50 times more massive than the Sun and have surface temperatures of 30,000°C. But these stellar spendthrifts will exhaust their nuclear fuel in a few million years. (See Chapter 7 for more on star variations.)

Nuclear energy is generated deep within the interior of our star, taking millions of years to percolate up to the Sun's visible surface, the *photosphere*. After this energy radiates from the photosphere as photons, it requires only about eight minutes for the Sun's light to reach the Earth, at a distance of 150,000,000 km.

The photosphere's diameter is about 1,400,000 km and its temperature is more than 6,000°C (about 10,000°F). If a chunk of even the most heat-resistant material were exposed to the temperatures of the Sun's visible surface, it would vaporize instantly—even before it reached the surface.

Above the visible photosphere are two other distinct solar layers, which are only visible when the Sun is eclipsed by the new Moon or through special solar telescopes in which artificial eclipses are created optically. The lower layer is the *chromosphere*, which is often called the Sun's lower atmosphere. The chromosphere extends only a few thousand kilometers above the photosphere. Above the chromosphere is the more tenuous and much hotter *corona*. The highly variable corona can extend 700,000 km or more above the chromosphere. The layers of the Sun are shown in Figure 5-1.

Figure 5-1. *Layers of the Sun.*

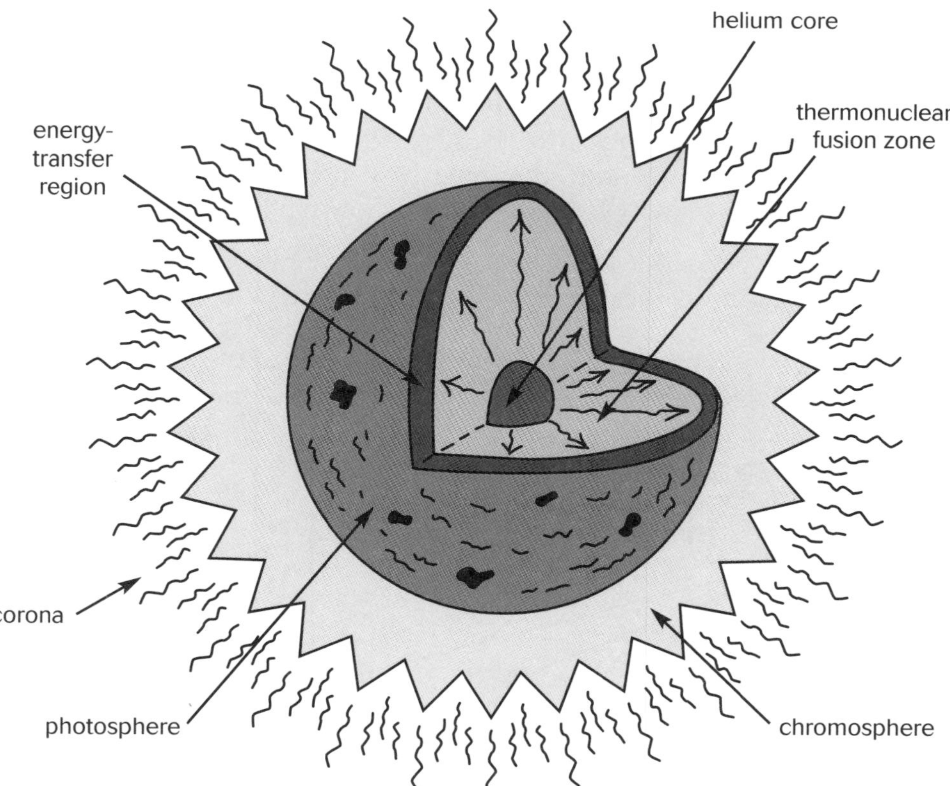

The mass of the Sun is about 1,000 times that of Jupiter, the most massive of the planets, and more than 300,000 times the mass of the Earth. In fact, if all the material of the solar system—planets, satellites, asteroids, and comets—were gathered together, the Sun would still be more than 500 times as massive. In terms of volume, about one million Earths could fit within our Sun.

For centuries, astronomers using protective equipment have monitored the motions of *sunspots* (which look like dark spots on the photosphere). From these studies, we've learned that the fluid mass of the Sun's photosphere rotates at different rates at different latitudes. A sunspot near the Sun's equator requires about 25 days to rotate once around the solar axis; the rotation rate near the poles is closer to 30 days.

Observing the Sun

When observing the Sun, remember that *you should never look directly at the Sun either with the naked eye or through a telescope*. The first telescopic astronomer, Galileo (1564–1642) damaged his vision, while observing sunspots.

For some telescopes, you can purchase something called a neutral-density filter that fits snuggly over your telescope's aperture and block's most of the sunlight. These can be expensive. *Never, never substitute a solar eyepiece filter for a solar aperture filter*. Even the slightest light leak in such a device can ruin your vision.

One safe approach to solar observing is to use a projection screen, as I described in *Telescope Power* (Wiley, 1993). As shown in Figure 5-2, a projection

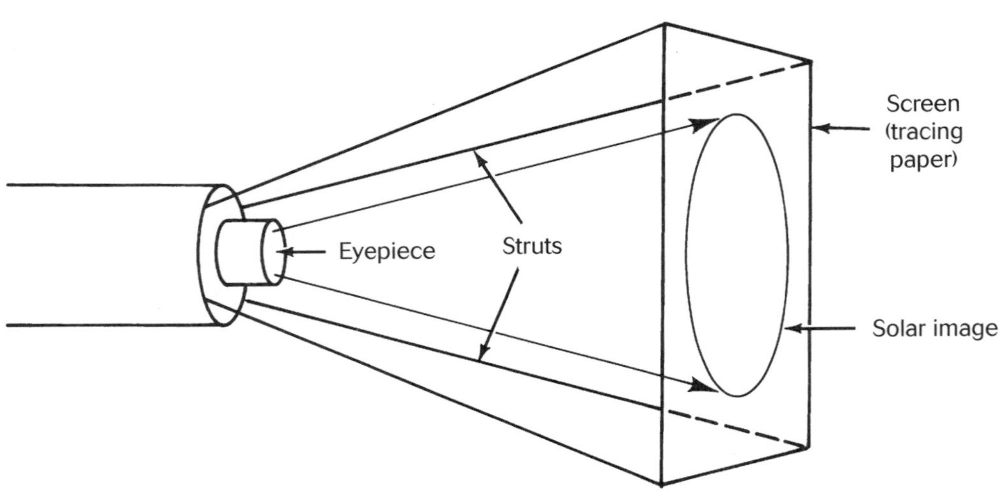

Figure 5-2. *A projection screen for safe solar viewing.*

screen consists of light paper, such as tracing paper, mounted to the eyepiece with a series of plywood struts. The struts can be attached to the eyepiece using wire, rubber bands, or a gripping material such as Velcro. The challenge in projection screen construction is to ensure that the screen does not fall from the eyepiece as you track the Sun across the sky. You may also want to cover the entire screen-supported structure with black cloth so that stray light doesn't reduce the contrast of your solar image.

Before attaching your projection screen to the telescope eyepiece, it's a good idea to focus your telescope on a distant object. Try not to change the focus as you attach the solar projection screen.

You may need to practice keeping the Sun in the telescope eyepiece without looking at the Sun. Observe the shadow cast on the ground by the telescope and projection screen as you alter the telescope's pointing direction. When the shadow is smallest, the Sun is centered in your telescope's field of view (FOV).

ACTIVITY 5-1

The Sun's Spectrum

Using an inexpensive handheld spectroscope (which can be purchased from your local planetarium or science center) and the eyepiece-mounted projection screen described above, you should be able to observe the Sun's spectum. Point the spectroscope at the solar image on your projection screen. Notice that the Sun's light is broken down into a colorful rainbow or *spectrum*. What color of the Sun's spectrum seems to be brightest through the spectroscope?

More elaborate spectroscopes mounted on large telescopes can detect the *spectral signatures* of hydrogen and other elements in the Sun's visible layers. (Each element has a characteristic spectrum.) Spectroscopy has given us valuable information about the composition and temperature of the Sun's layers.

The Solar Interior

Like other stars that formed at about the same time, the Sun is made up principally of the two lightest elements: hydrogen and helium. Our Sun is about 80 percent hydrogen and 20 percent helium, with a smattering of everything else.

Although the Sun is very hot at the photosphere, *temperature* (a measure of an object's internal energy) increases dramatically deeper into the solar interior.

The Mythological Sun

The Sun has figured in the mythological traditions of every human culture. In most ancient mythologies, the Sun was honored as either the most important sky god or the chief deity.

One essential concern to early agricultural societies was the apparent motion of the Sun. We know today that this is caused by the Earth's rotation about its axis and revolution around our star, the Sun. But to a Neolithic herdsman in Kush (now northern Sudan) or the wife of a farmer in Bronze Age Crete, the cause of solar motion was unknown.

The ancient Egyptians noticed that the Sun moved across the sky like a bird. They therefore pictured our star as equipped with fiery feathers and moving across the sky as a winged disk. Ancient Assyrians and Persians took this model one step further and equipped the winged solar disk with birdlike tail feathers. In an alternative Egyptian model, the sun god Ra is crowned with the Sun's fiery disk and he steers through the celestial realm aboard a magical boat.

People in ancient Greece and India, and later the Vikings of northern Europe, who rode horse-drawn chariots, thought the moving Sun was shaped like the wheels of a chariot and that it rolled across the sky.

To the Chumash native people of California, the Sun traveled across the sky on foot following a cord that traversed the Earth. The Karraru aborigines of Australia agreed that the Sun traveled by foot, but they identified our star with Karraru, a sky goddess.

The same is true for *pressure* (force per unit area) and *density* (mass per unit volume).

Deep within our star, a level of temperature, pressure, and density is reached at which *thermonuclear fusion* (a process by which light atomic nuclei combine to release energy) can occur. In this solar furnace, hydrogen atoms (actually the nuclei of these atoms) are converted into helium and energy. Inert helium "ash" falls toward the solar core. The energy percolates upward. High-energy photons produced in the solar furnace heat the gases in layers above the thermonuclear fusion zone. Some of the energy emitted by the Sun is in the form of ghostlike particles called *neutrinos* that react very slowly with matter and are therefore very hard to detect.

Below the photosphere, hot gas from the Sun's interior rises in a manner similar to carbonation in a glass of soda. These "bubbles" give the photosphere a granulated appearance when viewed under high magnification. Typical granules have a lifetime measured in minutes. As these granulation bubbles burst at the photosphere, some of their energy is transferred to the chromosphere and corona; most is radiated into space as sunlight.

Neutrinos speed through the Sun in a few seconds at the speed of light. The energy radiated toward Earth as solar photons requires millions of years to slowly percolate up to the photosphere from the Sun's thermonuclear furnace. But after leaving the photosphere, both neutrinos and photons require only about eight minutes to reach the Earth.

The Active Sun and the Earth

Our Sun has been stable enough for life on Earth to have survived for billions of years. But it should not be supposed that the Sun never changes.

On the visible face of the photosphere, amateur astronomers can view one aspect of solar activity: sunspots. Sunspots, which are often larger than the Earth, appear somewhat darker than the surrounding photosphere because they are slightly cooler—but they're still pretty hot, at about 4,500°C.

The typical sunspot has a darker central region called the *umbra* and a less dark, outer region called the *penumbra*. Sunspots often come in groups and have a typical lifetime measured in weeks.

ACTIVITY 5-2

Using Sunspot Observations to Determine Solar Rotation

On the solar image on your projection screen or through your telescope's neutral-density filter, you will see sunspots as smudges on the Sun. If you tweak the telescope tube slightly to move the solar image, you will notice that the sunspots move with the Sun—which indicates that they are not defects in your equipment.

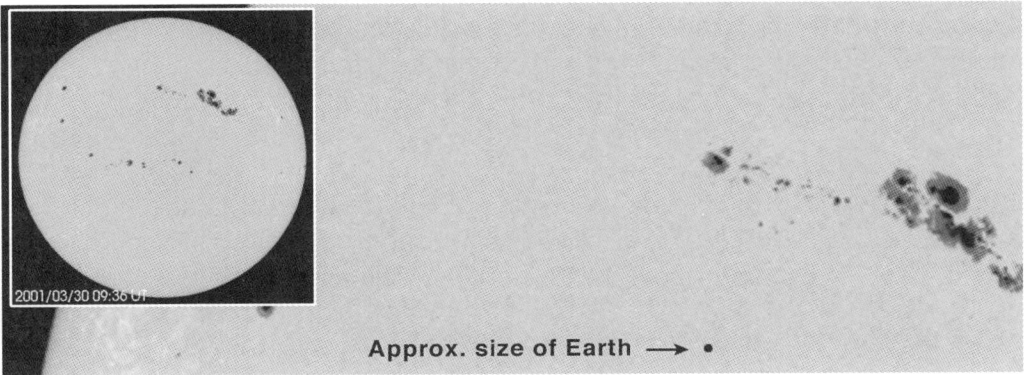

Figure 5-3. *Sunspots.*

If you draw a picture of the solar disk at intervals of a few days, you should be able to determine the motion of recognizable sunspot groups as the Sun rotates about its axis. A sunspot will cross the Sun's visible face in about two weeks. Can you detect any difference in rotation rate between sunspots close to and farther from the solar equator?

Sunspots are a measure of the solar activity cycle. During the 11-year solar cycle, the number of sunspots visible on the photosphere waxes and wanes. There are more sunspots during periods of peak solar activity.

During a *solar maximum* period, *solar flares* (eruptions of photospheric material) as well as many sunspots occur on the solar disk (see Figure 5-4). During an intense solar flare, the amount of solar material ejected into the interplanetary medium, the solar wind, increases. If a solar flare is directed toward the Earth, radiation levels in the Earth's upper atmosphere and in low Earth orbit may increase significantly, requiring astronauts and aviators to take protective measures. The northern and southern auroras may also become visible at unusually low latitudes because of the greater influx of high-energy electrically charged particles emitted from the Sun during a solar flare. (The *auroras* are produced when solar-wind particles are influenced by Earth's magnetic field as they enter the Earth's upper atmosphere in the polar regions. These displays are commonly referred to as the northern lights, or aurora borealis, and the southern lights, or aurora australis. Related to the flare is the prominence, a magnetically confined arch of gas near the Sun's rim.)

ACTIVITY 5-3

Monitoring Solar Activity

If you count both the number of sunspots visible on the solar surface (S) and the number of sunspot groups (G), you can estimate variations in solar activity by calculating N, the number of sunspots, using the following equation:

$$N = 10G + S$$

You may wish to compare your value of N with the daily values published each month in *Sky & Telescope.* Daily sunspot numbers are also available on the World Wide Web at www.oma.be/KSB-ORB/SIDC/index.html.

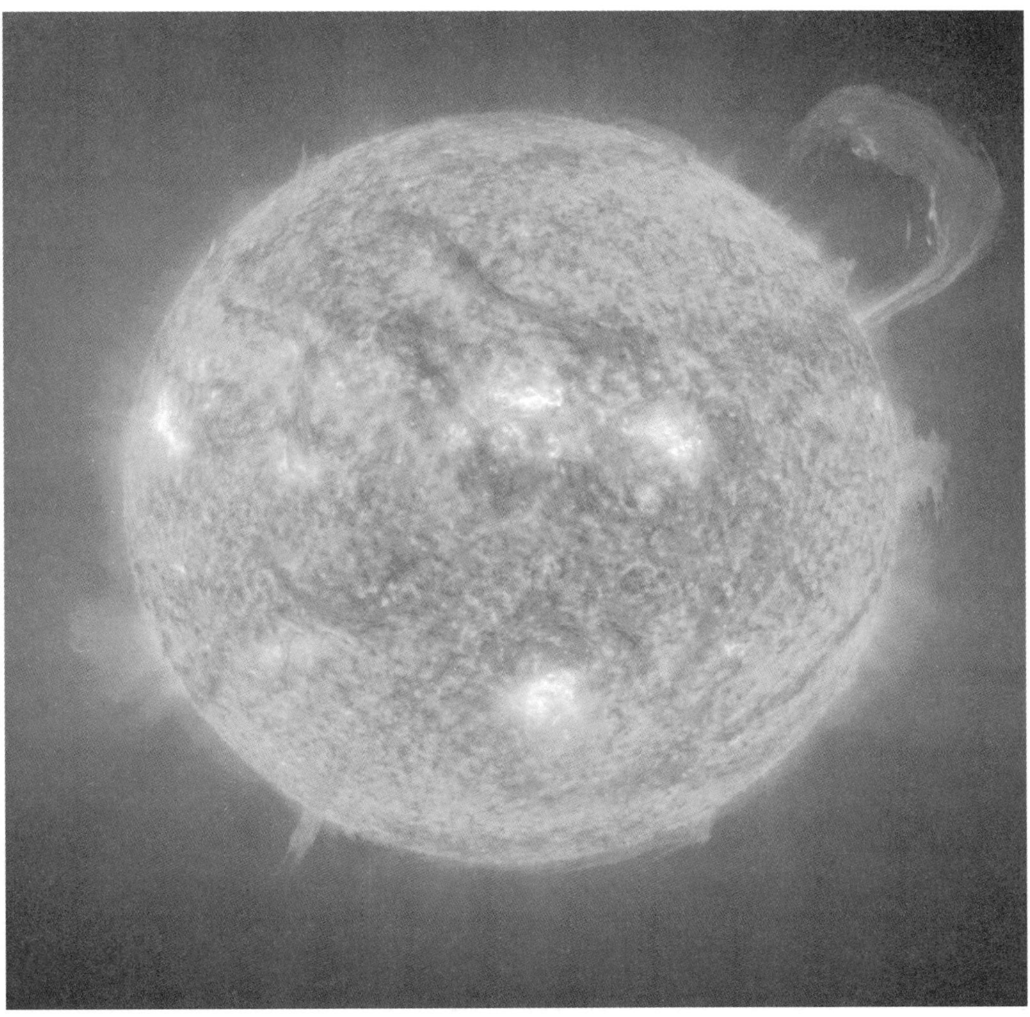

Figure 5-4. *Solar flares.*

Solar Energy

In a sense, almost all terrestrial *energy* (the ability to do work) comes from the Sun. When we burn a log in a fireplace, we are releasing energy originally from the Sun that was stored by photosynthesis during the tree's lifetime. Our cars use gasoline and our home furnaces use energy that came from the Sun, was stored in very ancient forests, and then was gradually converted to fossil fuels by geological processes.

Only the energy released by the splitting of massive atoms, such as uranium in nuclear fission reactors, does not have its source in the Sun. An older star near the nebula in which the Sun and the solar system formed produced this and other heavy elements (such as lead and thorium) during the supernova explosion that destroyed it.

The Sun's Future

As the Sun has matured, it has converted more and more of its hydrogen to helium. Since its birth almost five billion years ago, the Sun has gradually radiated increasing amounts of energy.

In perhaps two billion years, the increased flux in solar energy will begin to affect Earth's habitability. Eventually, unless corrective measures are taken (such as huge, orbiting sunscreens), increased heat will render our planet uninhabitable. If humans or their descendants survive in that remote era, they may choose to migrate to Mars or the moons of Jupiter to escape the rays of the expanding Sun.

But such measures will only be of temporary benefit. In about five billion years, the Sun's inert core will have grown so much that increased density and temperature in the core will cause the thermonuclear burning of helium and other formerly inert nuclei.

Solar expansion will then proceed at a greater pace. The Sun will consume Mercury and possibly Venus. In some models, the photosphere of the bloated Sun will even engulf the orbit of the Earth.

As a bloated, bright *giant star,* the Sun will consume its remaining nuclear resources at a prodigious rate. After 100 million years or so, it will begin to contract as internal fuels run out. The Sun will eventually end its career as a dim, shrunken *white dwarf* star barely the size of our Moon. But by that time, humans or their descendants will have left the solar system to find new homes in the far reaches of galactic space.

★6★

The Planets

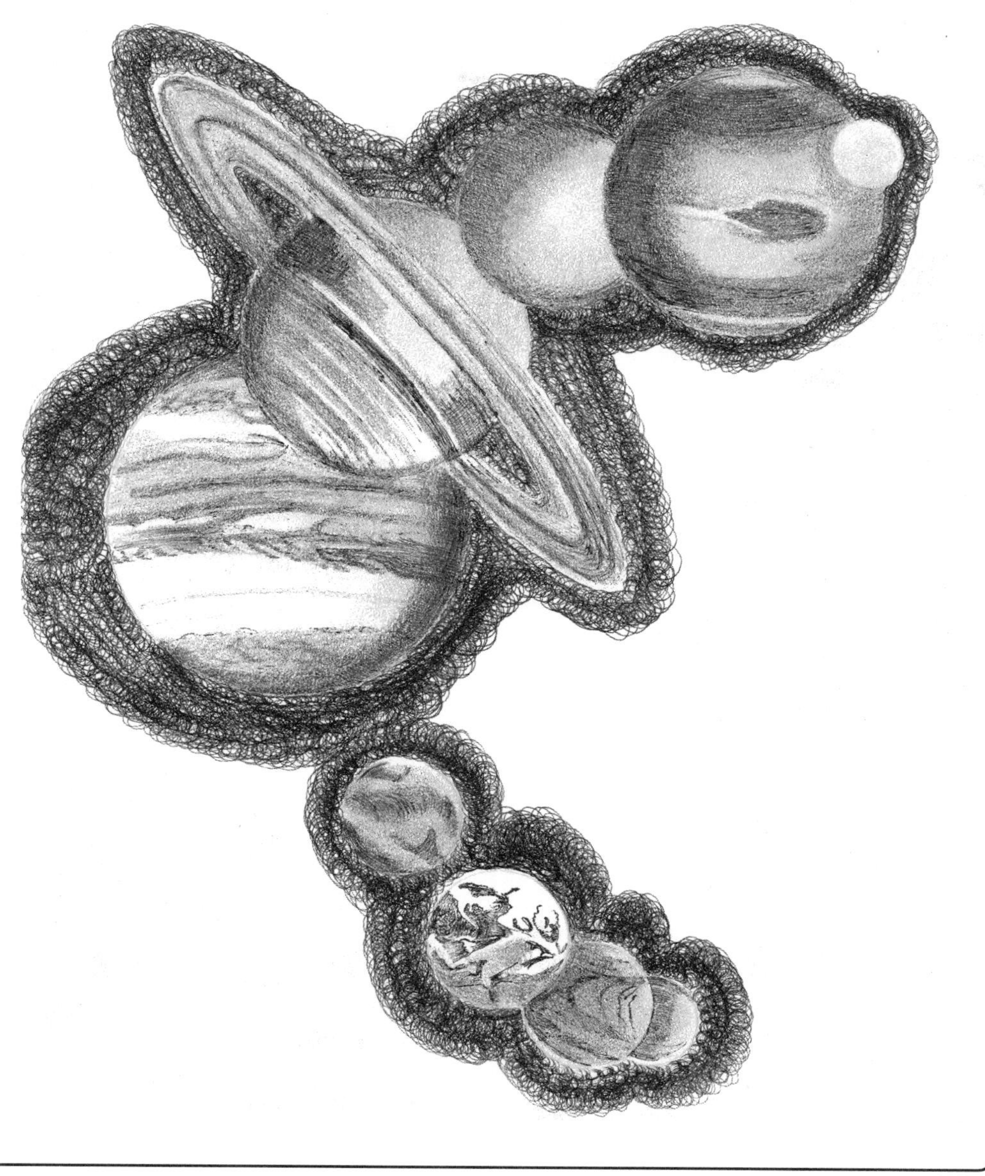

Our solar system contains nine planets—or perhaps only eight if you don't count Pluto as a planet. The five nearest the Sun (excluding the Earth) are visible to the naked eye, and four of these are easily observable through your telescope.

In order from the Sun, the planets are Mercury, Venus, Earth, Mars, Jupiter, Saturn, Uranus, Neptune, and Pluto. To the ancients, the naked-eye planets Mercury, Venus, Mars, Jupiter, and Saturn were considered "wandering stars" (the word *planet* meant comes from the Greek for "wanderer") because their positions measured against the fixed stars changed with time. To modern astronomers, a planet is an object that is larger than a comet or an asteroid, orbits a star, and shines by reflected light.

The Planets in History

Because the naked-eye planets rival or exceed bright stars in visibility, they became significant to sky watchers early in human history. Of special interest and importance were attempts to understand planetary motions.

The first known systematic observers of planetary motions were the Babylonians, about 3,000 years ago. They mounted multistory observation towers, called ziggurats, and plotted the positions of the visible naked-eye planets against the background of fixed stars.

The careful observations of the Babylonians allowed the classical Greek philosophers who followed them to derive theoretical models of the solar system, called *cosmogonies*, around 2,500 years ago.

All three of the Greek cosmogonies were correct in assuming that the Moon orbits the Earth. They also correctly assumed that the Sun was more distant from the Earth than is the Moon and were able to explain eclipses.

But they also had to explain why the planets move in one direction across the sky most of the time (*posigrade motion*) but sometimes stop and loop back (*retrograde motion*). The earliest Greek cosmogony, that of Pythagoras, was least successful in explaining planetary motions. Pythagoras assumed that the Earth was stationary in the middle of the cosmos. The Moon orbited the Earth as did the more distant Sun. Revolving around the moving Sun were the naked-eye planets.

Slightly more successful (but still incorrect) was the *geocentric model*, which also placed the Earth at the center of creation. Closest to the Earth was the Moon, followed by Mercury and then Venus. The Sun was next. Beyond the Sun were the *superior planets* (planets farther from the Sun than Earth is), Mars, Jupiter, and Saturn. All motions were along perfectly circular tracks. Occasional retrograde motions were explained by loops called *epicycles* that were built into the planetary tracks.

Many famous figures contributed to the theoretical development of the geocentric worldview. These included the philosopher Aristotle (384–322 B.C.), the astronomer Ptolemy (second century A.D.), and the philosopher Hypatia (c. 370–415), who was the first woman astonomer we know of.

Competing with the geocentric cosmogony was the *heliocentric model,* which placed the Sun in the center of the solar system. Orbiting the Sun were Mercury, Venus, Earth, Mars, Jupiter, and Saturn. The Moon orbited the Earth. In the classical Greek version of the heliocentric worldview, all planetary motions were circular. Some epicycles were eliminated since they could be explained by relative motion of Earth and other planets around the Sun, but some were still necessary because of the requirement for perfectly circular planetary motions.

Although late classical and early Christian sky observers could not prove either the geocentric or heliocentric models, the geocentric cosmogony was favored by the Catholic Church.

In the Middle Ages, Islamic observers developed better naked-eye observing tools and noted that the geocentric worldview was becoming very complex. It wasn't until the Renaissance that these observations became available to Europeans. The Polish astronomer Nicolaus Copernicus (1473–1543) argued that the increased complexity of the geocentric worldview meant that the heliocentric model was probably correct.

Using obervations of Mars by Tycho Brahe (1546–1601), Johannes Kepler (1571–1630) developed a version of the heliocentric cosmogony in which the planets moved in elliptical paths around the Sun. When closest to the Sun in this model (at perihelion), a planet moved faster than when it was most distant (at aphelion). Kepler did away with the epicycles and derived a formula relating a planet's orbital period to its distance from the Sun.

Galileo Galilei (1564–1642), who lived in northern Italy, was the first person to turn a telescope to the heavens. His observations of the phases of Venus

Naming the Planets

The planet names we use today are based on Greek mythology. Mercury was named for the god Mercury, who ran the celestial messenger service, carrying communiqués between various gods and between gods and mortals. Venus is named after the goddess of love. Because of its bloodred color, Mars was named for the god of war.

Huge, stately Jupiter, which is more massive than the rest of the solar system (excluding the Sun) combined, derives its name from the king of the classical gods.

Saturn, which takes the longest time to revolve around the Sun, derives its name from the god of time.

and the satellites of Jupiter helped sway the astronomical jury (although not the Catholic Church) toward acceptance of Kepler's version of the heliocentric model. Born the year that Galileo died, the British mathematician Isaac Newton (1642–1727) developed the basis of modern physics. Newtonian mechanics and gravity theory successfully explained the elliptical motions of the planets.

With the exception of tiny, distant Pluto, all the planets of our solar system orbit in approximately the same plane, called the ecliptic. This is the apparent path of the Sun and planets across the sky. All planets in our solar system, also with the exception of Pluto, have nearly circular orbits. Appendix D gives data on the planets, such as distance from the Sun, revolution rate, and mass. Note that Mercury, the closest planet to the Sun, orbits at an average distance of about 0.4 AU from the Sun, Earth is at 1 AU from the Sun, and frigid Pluto orbits at about 40 AU from the Sun.

ACTIVITY 6-1

A Scale Model of Solar-System Distances and Planet Sizes

As a memorial to its famous resident, the astronomer Carl Sagan (1934–1996), the city of Ithaca in central New York state has constructed a scale model of the solar system. Starting from the "Sun," located at a pylon near the center of town, you can walk a few paces to the simulated orbit of Mercury. Venus is about twice as far from the Sun as Mercury, and Earth is a little more distant; Pluto is blocks away.

You can easily create a smaller scale model of solar-system distances and planet sizes on a tabletop or floor. All you need are some small pebbles to serve as the planets and a metric ruler.

Refer to the table of planet data in Appendix D. Let 1 AU = 10 cm on your metric ruler. The central marker represents the Sun. The orbit of Mercury will be 4 mm from the Sun, Venus 7 mm, and Earth 1 cm. Pluto's orbit will be 40 cm from the Sun, 40 times the Earth-Sun separation.

If you refer again to Appendix D, you'll see that Pluto's diameter is one-fifth that of the Earth and that Jupiter's diameter is 11 times that of the Earth. If you have different sized rocks or balls of modeling clay, a 1-mm-diameter object can be used to model Pluto. Earth will be 5 mm in diameter. On this scale, the largest planet, Jupiter, will have a diameter of 5.5 cm.

Types of Planets

A number of different characterizations are used to consider the planets of our solar system. As mentioned above, worlds out to Saturn are classified as *naked-eye planets* because they were known to pretelescopic sky observers. Uranus, Neptune, and Pluto are *telescopic planets* because these worlds were discovered with the aid of this instrument.

Planets closer to the Sun than the Earth—Mercury and Venus—are called *inferior planets*. Because of their position between the Earth and the Sun, inferior planets present a cycle of phases. The superior planets are farther from the Sun than the Earth is. They are always visible from Earth in full phase.

The inner four planets—Mercury, Venus, Earth, and Mars—are close enough to the Sun that their early evolution was affected by light and particles emitted by our star. These *terrestrial planets* are all comparatively small and rocky, have relatively thin atmospheres, and are accompanied by at most a few natural satellites. The next four planets—Jupiter, Saturn, Uranus, and Neptune— are the *gas giants* or *Jovians*. All of these planets are comparatively large, have dense atmospheres and many satellites, and are accompanied by ring systems.

Distant, tiny Pluto revolves around the Sun in the most elliptical of the planetary orbits and with the highest inclination to the ecliptic of all solar-system planets. Many astronomers now believe that Pluto should be classified as the largest of the icy Kuiper belt cometoids rather than the smallest of the planets.

Another type of object has been discovered orbiting some nearby stars. These *brown dwarfs* are more massive than the Jovians and are intermediate in size between planets and stars. Using the Hubble Space Telescope, astronomers have succeeded in imaging the nearest member of this strange new substellar category.

Viewing the Planets

Three and a half centuries after Newton's birth, his physics and Galileo's telescope have taught us a lot about our celestial neighbors. All the planets have unique properties and interesting features to observe. The easiest to observe are Venus, Mars, Jupiter, and Saturn.

Look in the western sky after sunset or to the east before sunrise. The brightest objects in that part of the sky (excluding the Moon) are probably planets. To locate planets visible in the sky for any date, consult a monthly astronomical publication such as *Astronomy* or *Sky & Telescope*.

Figure 6-1. *Mercury.*

Mercury

Closest to the Sun, at 0.39 AU, Mercury is too small ever to have held an atmosphere or ocean. Mercury has about 5 percent the mass of the Earth, rotates once every 59 days, and revolves around the Sun once every 88 days. You would weigh about 40 percent of your weight on Earth if you were standing on the crater-pocked surface of this small world. Mercury's diameter is about 4,800 km.

During the long Mercurian night, temperatures on the planet's surface fall to about –200°C. But after the sun rises, the surface temperatures can reach 400°C. In spite of the enormous fluctuations in daytime temperatures, astronomers bouncing radar beams off Mercury and observing the reflected beams have found indications of frozen water near Mercury's poles. This ice may have been deposited in deep craters shielded from the Sun that were created by ancient cometary impacts.

There is no life now on Mercury, and life has almost certainly always been absent from that sunbaked and airless planet. Close-up images of the planet's surface were obtained from the *Mariner 10* spacecraft, which flew by Mercury during the 1970s.

ACTIVITY 6-2

Observing Mercury

Even in the unpolluted skies of the ancient world, observing Mercury was a challenge. The planet is always very close to the Sun and can therefore be viewed only shortly before sunrise or shortly after sunset. If you live under unpolluted skies and are up to the challenge, check the monthly astronomy magazines for the best Mercury-observing opportunities.

Mercury will seem yellow or red in color. With a blue filter and a telescope aperture of 7.5 cm or greater, you may see some surface detail. Under most conditions, you will observe a crescent Mercury.

Venus

The second planet from the Sun, at 0.7 AU, Venus (see Figure 6-2) is a near twin of the Earth in terms of size. Its diameter is slightly smaller than that of the Earth; you would weigh 90 percent of your Earth weight on the surface of Venus. The Venusian solar year is about one-third shorter than the Earth year.

Figure. 6-2. *The surface of Venus, pieced together from images obtained by the* Magellan *spacecraft in 1992.*

For centuries, telescopic astronomers have observed this bright, cloud-shrouded world and wondered what went on below the perpetual Venusian cloud cover. Might the clouds consist of water, and might they cover a planetwide swamp inhabited by dinosaurs? Or might this planet's dense atmosphere instead hide a blistering hot surface totally hostile to life as we know it?

Probes from Earth began visiting our sister world in 1962. We soon learned that Venus is an inferno. Because there is so much infrared-absorbing carbon dioxide in Venus's atmosphere temperatures on the surface exceed the peak temperatures on Mercury. (*Infrared* is lower-energy electromagnetic radiation than visible light.) The atmosphere is largely carbon dioxide, and water seems to be absent. If this weren't bad enough, the atmospheric pressure at the surface of Venus is perhaps 90 times greater than that at the surface of Earth. An atmospheric acid layer is also not a good thing (from the viewpoint of short-lived probes we have deposited on Venus's surface), and intense volcanism refashions the planet's surface at intervals of millions of years.

ACTIVITY 6-3

Observing the Atmosphere of Venus

Note that Venus, like Mercury, can only be observed after sunset or before dawn because of its proximity to the Sun. Although your telescope will not be able to penetrate the dense atmosphere of Venus, you may be able to observe some atmospheric effects. Try sketching the planet's image on succeeding evening (or predawn) observing sessions. Include the terminator—the boundary between dark and light on the planet's surface. Can you detect any near-terminator variations in brightness on sketches made during different observing sessions? Some astronomers have noted occasional brightenings near the ends of Venus' crescent.

Planetary probes have also taught us that Venus rotates in the opposite direction of its solar revolution and that its day is somewhat longer than its year. Because of its relative proximity to the Earth, space enthusiasts wonder if humans will ever live on Venus. Although the task is not impossible, *terraforming* this world—making it more Earth-like—would be a major technological challenge for future humanity. Venus now has a number of artificial satellites that originated from Earth, but like Mercury, no known natural satellites attend Venus.

ACTIVITY 6-4

Observing Venus's Phases and Changes in Size

As Venus and the Earth orbit the Sun, you will see different phases of our sister planet like the phases of the Moon. Venus is brightest in crescent phase, when it is about six times brighter than the brightest star.

The solar revolution of Earth and Venus also causes Venus's angular size to vary. You can keep track of these changes if you observe Venus through a reticle eyepiece. (See Appendix B for information on using a reticle eyepiece.)

Mars

At an average distance of 1.52 AU from the Sun, Mars (see Figure 6-3) orbits our star in a little less than two Earth years. However, future Mars visitors and colonists will be glad to know that this world completes one rotation about its axis in almost precisely 24 hours. The Martian day is almost exactly equal to the terrestrial day.

Mars is a smaller world than the Earth, with about one-tenth the Earth's mass and half its diameter. If transported to Mars's surface without a spacesuit (not a good idea), you would weigh 38 percent of your weight on Earth.

Mars is far from being a terrestrial paradise. Temperatures vary from near freezing at high noon during Martian summer to a brisk –100°C during winter nights. Like the Earth, Mars has polar ice caps—but they are made of frozen carbon dioxide as well as frozen water.

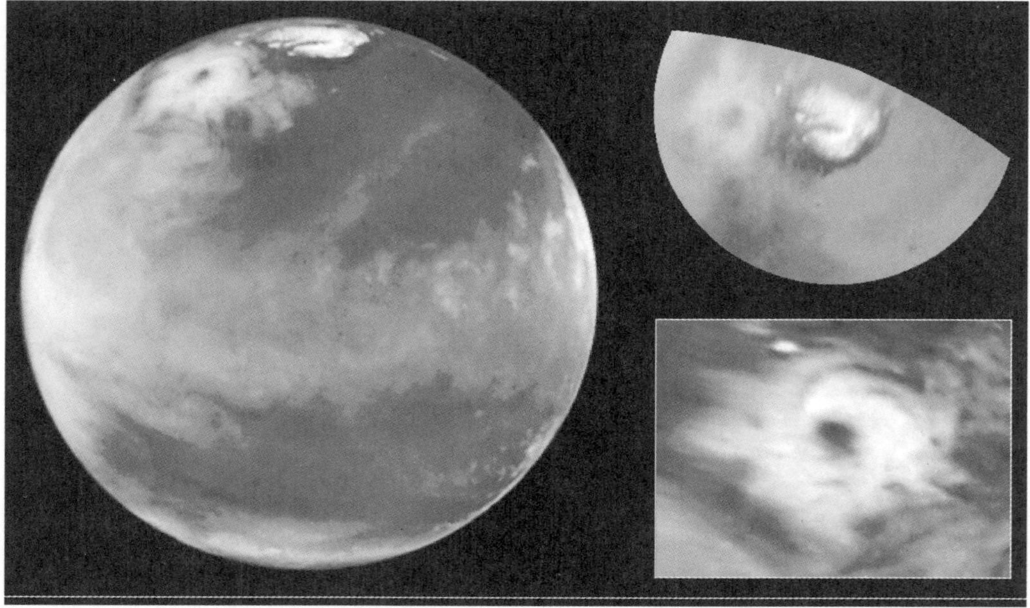

Figure 6-3. *A Martian polar storm.*

ACTIVITY 6-5

Coordinated Mars Observations

The Red Planet has become a favorite target for robotic space missions. Try observing this neighbor world while a mission is en route to check for any variation in surface features or atmosphere. One thing to look for is development of global dust storms. When these occur, visibility of surface features decreases. Dust storms decrease the contrast of photographic images taken from Mars orbit and could interfere with landing attempts. For the latest information on U.S.-launched Mars missions, consult http://www.nasa.gov/, the NASA web site. A web search will reveal addresses of non-U.S. space agencies conducting interplanetary missions.

Mars's crimson-red color is due to an oxidized surface layer—perhaps it is fair to say that Mars has rusted. Scientists theorize that solar ultraviolet photons produce oxygen atoms from Martian carbon dioxide and water vapor. These oxygen atoms react quickly with the Martian soil.

Some Martian features change with the seasons. While early telescopic astronomers believed that these seasonal variations were caused by vegetation, we know today that windblown dust is the probable explanation. Although the pressure of Mars's mostly carbon dioxide atmosphere is about 1 percent that of the Earth's atmosphere, wind speeds well in excess of 60 km per hour can readily push Mars's surface dust around. When Mars is closest to the Sun, planetwide dust storms are often raised. These can greatly hinder observations of Mars from both Earth and spacecraft.

In addition to dust dunes and polar ice caps, Mars has many other fascinating surface features (see Figures 6-4A and B). There are many impact craters, volcanoes much higher than Everest, which could fill

Figure 6-4A. *Martian surface feature Olympus Mons is taller than three Mount Everests.*

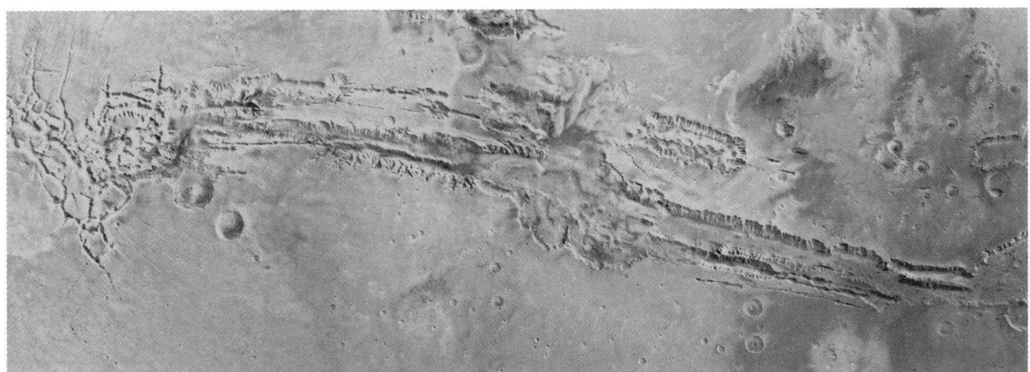

Figure 6-4B. *Valles Marineris, a Martian canyon system over 3,000 km long and 8 km deep.*

much of California if moved to Earth, and a rift valley that dwarfs the Grand Canyon. Early observations of the Great Rift Valley of Mars may have contributed to the now-abandoned theory that intelligent Martians had constructed a planetary network of canals.

ACTIVITY 6-6

Atmospheric Variation and Mars's Canals

Since terrestrial observers must look through the atmospheres of two planets when they observe the surface of Mars, various types of optical illusions may have contributed to the fallacy of the Martian canals. Experiments have revealed that observers concentrating on observing a nonuniform surface at the limits of visibility often "connect the dots" and report nonexistent straight lines. Try observing Mars and sketching its appearance when it is closest to Earth (when Mars and Earth are at *opposition,* or opposite each other) under successively higher magnification and with different color filters. Can you see the canals?

If you were standing on the Martian surface at night, you would see two moving celestial objects. These are the two small satellites of Mars—Phobos and Deimos, named for the attendants of the ancient war god. Probably captured asteroids or cometary nuclei, these heavily cratered objects measure 20 to 30 km in diameter. They may some day serve as convenient space stations for visiting ships from Earth.

Although spacecraft that have landed on the planet's surface have found no signs of present-day Martians, some astronomers speculate that life may exist in geologically warmed subsurface regions. In such "warm pockets," the frozen water thought to underlie the Martian surface may have melted and life may thrive. There may not have been artificial canals on Mars, but orbiting probes have imaged the remains of ancient rivers and oceans. Mars may once have been warm and wet and teeming with life.

Recent studies of meteorites ejected from Mars during impacts or eruptions and later deposited on Earth indicate the possible presence of ancient Martian microorganisms. It is even possible that Martian life originated first and was transported to Earth to seed our planet. We may all be Martians.

Whether or not life presently exists upon the surface of the Red Planet, few astronomers doubt that it will be there soon. A round trip to Mars would take two to three years using early-twenty-first-century technology.

JUPITER

At 318 times the Earth's mass and more than 11 times the Earth's diameter, Jupiter (see Figure 6-5) is indeed the king of the planets. In spite of its gargantuan proportions, this world rotates once around its axis in about 10 hours. Since Jupiter is 5.2 AU from the Sun, its year is much longer than that of the inner planets. Jupiter revolves around the Sun once every 12 years.

Because of the large size of this planet, you would weigh a lot on its visible surface—about two and a half times what you weigh on Earth. But what we perceive as the surface of Jupiter is actually the top of its enormous atmosphere—if Jupiter has a rocky core, it is very deep beneath the visible cloud layer.

Jupiter is brighter than any celestial object other than the Moon and Venus, and is a fun target for observation. Jupiter's brightness and its wonderful colors are due to cloud bands in its mostly hydrogen-helium atmosphere. The varying colors may be caused by impurities in the Jovian atmosphere.

Like all the giant planets, Jupiter is circled by a ring of fine dust and ice particles. Unfortunately, the Jovian rings are very dim and tenuous and therefore not visible in your telescope. Jupiter's intense magnetic field interacts with the solar wind to result in radiation belts and it emits energy in the *radio* (lowest-frequency) waveband of the spectrum (perhaps as a result of atmospheric lightning). Jupiter is attended by many satellites. Four of these—Callisto, Europa, Io, and Ganymede—are easily viewed through binoculars or a small telescope.

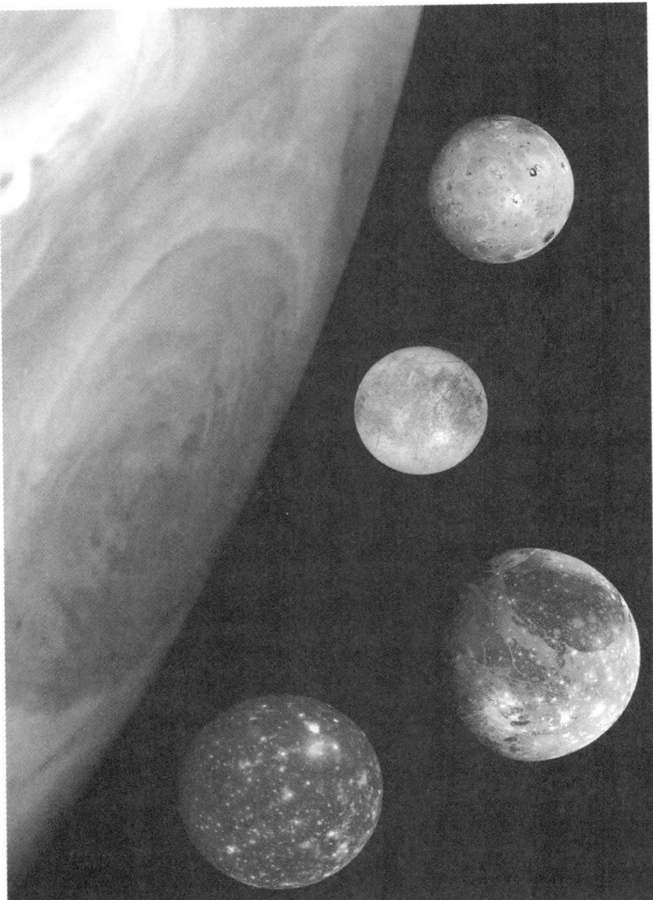

Figure 6-5.
A composite image of Jupiter and its four largest moons. From top right, the moons are Io, Europa, Ganymede, and Callisto.

ACTIVITY 6-7

Observing the Jovian Moons with a Reticle Eyepiece

Try observing Jupiter and its four large moons through your reticle eyepiece. If you have calibrated this eyepiece as described in Appendix B, you can determine the angular separation between the planet and each of its large satellites.

You will observe these large satellites strung along the same plane around Jupiter like a miniature solar system. If one of the satellites is missing, it is passing either in front of or behind the giant planet.

Try repeating your reticle eyepiece observations of Jupiter's large satellites on succeeding nights and sketching the positions of the planet and satellites. Io will have moved most and Callisto least. Can you identify the large moons of Jupiter?

The large Jovian satellites are worlds in their own right. Europa is 65 percent the mass of our Moon. The other three are considerably larger than Earth's natural satellite. Ganymede is twice the mass of the Moon. Io is closest to Jupiter and revolves around the planet every 1.77 days. Europa orbits Jupiter every 3.55 Earth days; more distant Ganymede and Callisto require 7.16 and 16.7 days respectively to complete one revolution.

Ganymede is the brightest and Callisto the dimmest of the Jovian satellites. Were it not for the proximity of the bright giant planet, these moons would just barely be visible to the naked eye for people with excellent eyesight during ideal observing conditions.

ACTIVITY 6-8

Identifying the Large Moons of Jupiter by Brightness

When you observe the large Jovian satellites through your telescope, you will notice that all of them are not always visible. Sometimes, one or more is eclipsed by the planet or is in transit (passing) across the face of Jupiter. Under good conditions, you may be able to see the shadow of a satellite in transit as it crosses in front of the planet's disk.

If all four satellites are in view, you can discriminate Ganymede as the brightest and Callisto as the dimmest. To tell the difference between the satellites of intermediate brightness—Europa and Io—you must also consider the moons' orbital periods around Jupiter.

Four probes from Earth—*Pioneer 10* and *11* and *Voyager 1* and *2*—have photographed Jupiter and its satellites as these craft flew by on their way out of the solar system. More recently, the *Galileo* probe has orbited the giant planet and deposited an instrument package in Jupiter's atmosphere.

It was only with the dawn of space exploration that scientists learned how diverse the large satellites of Jupiter are. Ganymede and Callisto are both covered by significant quantities of ice and geologically recent impact craters. Io has numerous erupting volcanoes, probably triggered by tides produced under its surface by nearby Jupiter. Europa is a most exciting world. It is apparently covered by an ocean of water tens of kilometers in depth. Although the Europan ocean is mostly frozen because of Jupiter's great distance from the Sun, there are indications that portions of the ocean consist of liquid water. During the twenty-first century, life-detecting probes will almost certainly be dispatched to this distant and tantalizing little world.

ACTIVITY 6-9

Filter and Reticle Observations of Jupiter's Cloud Bands and the Great Red Spot

When you've checked out the large Jovian satellites, you might turn your attention to the colorful horizontal Jovian cloud bands. Try to determine which of your color filters is best for observing various features of Jupiter's visible disk.

One particuliarly interesting feature of Jupiter's atmosphere is the Great Red Spot. Easily visible about midway between the planet's equator and south pole, this feature is so large that it could easily swallow the Earth. The Great Red Spot may be a Jovian storm that has existed for at least three centuries. This feature is observed to slowly shift in longitude and latitude, as if it were suspended in Jupiter's atmosphere.

If you observe the visible surface of Jupiter (actually the cloud tops) through a reticle eyepiece, you can estimate the angular size of cloud bands and the Great Red Spot. Since Jupiter's equatorial radius is about 71,500 km, you might be able to estimate the physical size of these features.

Although the source of semipermanent turbulent eddies such as the Great Red Spot in the atmosphere of gas giant planets has long been a mystery, it might be explained by impacts. When portions of Comet Shoemaker-Levy 9 were observed to impact Jupiter in 1994, visible scars from the impacts persisted for days.

SATURN

The next planet out from the Sun is beautiful Saturn (see Figure 6-6). The only world in the solar system with an easily visible ring system, Saturn is 9.5 AU from the Sun. At this great distance, the planet revolves slowly—the Saturnian year is about 30 Earth years long. Although Saturn is smaller than Jupiter, its mass is still about 95 times that of the Earth.

In addition to its rings, Saturn is attended by many satellites. The largest, Titan, is visible in small telescopes and is the only solar-system satellite to have a dense atmosphere. The Cassini-Huygens mission probe, currently en route to Saturn, includes a Titan lander. The Titan landing attempt is scheduled to take place in 2004.

The most prominent feature of Saturn is its dramatic ring system. The rings are invisible when viewed end on, but they are thousands of kilometers across. The rings are most likely composed of rock and ice from an asteroid or comet that was pulled apart during a close Saturn approach.

Figure 6-6. *Saturn and three of its moons: Tethys, Dione, and Rhea (tiny bright spots to the left of the planet).*

ACTIVITY 6-10

Observing and Estimating the Size of Saturn's Rings

Saturn's equatorial radius is about 60,000 km. Using this information and a reticle eyepiece, try to estimate the size of Saturn's rings.

If your telescope has an aperture of at least 7.5 cm, you might be able to observe a gap in the rings called Cassini's division. Space probes have revealed many other ring gaps not visible from Earth. Small satellites orbit within the ring systems of the giant planets, gravitationally "herding" ring particles into certain positions and producing visible gaps.

You may observe color variations in the rings. These are caused by variations in the dust and ice particles that comprise this beautiful feature.

ACTIVITY 6-11

Observing Saturn through Color Filters

Perhaps because of Saturn's greater distance from the Sun, its atmosphere is much less colorful than Jupiter's. However, a patient observer in a good location can still discern some detail in Saturn's atmosphere.

Try observing Saturn under moderate magnification with different color filters attached to your telescope's eyepiece. Which filter is best for observing features of the planet's atmosphere?

Sometimes Saturn's rings occult a bright star. Scientists can study ring structure (particle density and composition) remotely by estimating how much the star dims as it passes behind the planet's rings and by observing the duration of the occultation. You can participate in such an "occultation event" by regularly reading the monthly astronomy magazines and planning your observing session accordingly.

Uranus

Traveling beyond Saturn, we come first to Uranus. Just visible to the naked eye, Uranus looks like a small greenish disk in telescopes of 7.5 cm or larger. Uranus is about 19 AU from the Sun and requires 84 years to orbit our star. This planet is almost 15 times as massive as the Earth, and it has many satellites and a ring system. Something big must have knocked this planet on its side early in the history of the solar system, since Uranus's axis of rotation is close to the plane of its revolution around the Sun.

Neptune

Neptune, the most distant of the gas giant worlds, is about 30 AU from the Sun and requires 165 years to orbit the Sun. Too dim to be seen with the naked eye, Neptune has a mass about 17 times that of the Earth. A magnification of 300 times or greater is needed to resolve Neptune's greenish disk. As with Uranus, the satellites and rings of this distant giant are observable from space probes and space telescopes, but not through amateur instruments.

Pluto

The most distant planet from the Sun is tiny Pluto, in an elliptical orbit with a maximum distance of almost 40 AU from the Sun. Pluto and its large moon, Charon, require almost 250 years to orbit the Sun. Sometimes this planet is closer to the Sun than Neptune is. Pluto was most recently within Neptune's orbit betwen 1979 and 1999 and will not return to perihelion for more than two centuries. Because of its small size (about 2,000 km in diameter), many astronomers consider Pluto a large cometlike member of the Kuiper belt rather than a true planet.

★7★

The Stars

You may devote most of your observing time to the Moon and the planets. But as an astronomer, you cannot help but be moved by the starry immensities beyond. What are the stars? Can we ever reach them? And what is beyond these bright, distant lights in the sky? People have asked these questions for millennia. But only today, with the aid of modern science, can we attempt an answer.

The Variety of Stars

The smallest stars that shine in our skies are less than 100 times as massive as the largest planets. The largest stars may have 100 times or more the Sun's mass. In size, small stars are of planetary dimension; giants would fill much of our solar system if they replaced the Sun. Stars go through predictable life cycles, from their birth in stellar nurseries to their eventual (sometimes spectacular) demise.

All stars are self-luminous, meaning that they create their own light. Middle-aged stars shine by light generated deep in their interior from thermonuclear reactions. Young stars, deep inside dusty stellar nurseries called *emission nebula*, shine by energy released when gravitationally attracted gas impacts the infant stars. Old stars have exhausted their store of thermonuclear fuel, but they are still dimly visible in large telecopes, shining from light emitted as outer-atmospheric gases collapse toward the shrunken core.

In all middle-aged stars, there is a balance between self-gravitation (which tends to make the star collapse) and the pressure of electromagnetic radiation released by thermonuclear processes deep in the stellar interior (which tends to make the star expand).

This balance is not always perfect. Some stars are *pulsating variables*, getting brighter and dimmer at different times. In these stars, the thermonuclear furnace slows, which causes the star to dim and collapse somewhat. This collapse in turn heats the star's interior and increases the star's themonuclear reaction rate, which causes the star to expand and brighten. Some pulsating variables are irregular in their oscillations (periodic changes in brightness). Others have such regular periods that astronomers can depend upon their radiant output. These *Cepheid* and *RR Lyrae variable* stars serve as celestial lighthouses—calibration aids to astronomers charting the far reaches of the universe.

The measure of star brightness has a long history. About 2,100 years ago, the Greek astronomer Hipparchus divided visible stars into six brightness levels and developed the scale of visible *apparent magnitude*. A 6th-magnitude star is barely visible to the unassisted human eye under ideal viewing conditions. Our eye receives about two and a half times as much luminous energy from a 5th-magnitude star. A 4th-magnitude star is about two and a half times as bright as a 5th-magnitude star, and so on. The brightest stars visible to the naked eye have magnitudes of about 0.

Another measure of star brightness is the *absolute magnitude* scale. Absolute magnitude corrects for star distance, so stars are rated not by how bright they seem but by how bright they would be if they were all at the same distance from the Sun—32.6 light-years.

The Significance of Star Colors

When you observe the night sky with the unassisted eye, binoculars, or your telescope, you cannot help but notice the variety of stellar colors. Some stars are blue, while others are red, yellow, or even green. Astronomers have learned that star color is indicative of surface temperature.

Although core temperatures are in the vicinity of 15,000,000°C for all mature stars, surface temperatures are more variable. The bluest stars have surface temperatures of 30,000°C or hotter. Yellow stars like the Sun have surface temperatures in the vicinity of 6,000°C, and the coolest, red stars have surface temperatures less than 3,000°C.

Star color and temperature are a measure of star lifetime and mass as well. Hot, blue, hydrogen-burning stars may be as much as 50 times more massive than the Sun. These tend to use up their store of hydrogen fuel in a few million years. Yellow stars of roughly solar mass can maintain their hydrogen fires for billions of years, and cool red stars, which may be one-tenth the Sun's mass, will burn hydrogen for as long as a trillion years.

Astrophysicists have developed a scheme to classify all stars according to color and size. This is called the *Hertzsprung-Russell (HR) diagram* (see Figure 7-1).

The vertical axis of the HR diagram represents absolute *stellar luminosity class* relative to the Sun. This means that if our Sun were replaced by another star, a dim red star would give us about one ten-thousandth as much light as the Sun while a very bright blue star would flood the Earth with a million times as much light as the Sun.

The horizontal axis represents *stellar spectral class* (surface temperature and color). In the late nineteenth century, astronomers classified stars according to the dark lines in their spectra, which indicated star temperature and composition. In order of decreasing surface temperature, stars belong to spectral classes O, B, A, F, G, K, and M. If you have trouble remembering this order, each spectral class is the first letter of a word in the sentence "Oh, Be A Fine Girl (or Guy), Kiss Me."

Notice the different stellar luminosity classes (or sizes) on the HR diagram. The most luminous stars are *supergiants*, followed by somewhat dimmer *giants*. Most stars are stable, *main-sequence stars*—hydrogen burners like the Sun. Dead,

Figure 7-1. *The Hertzsprung-Russell diagram. Stellar luminosity (L) is plotted versus stellar spectral class and surface temperature. Positions 1, 2, 3, and 4 are various evolutionary stages of the Sun.*

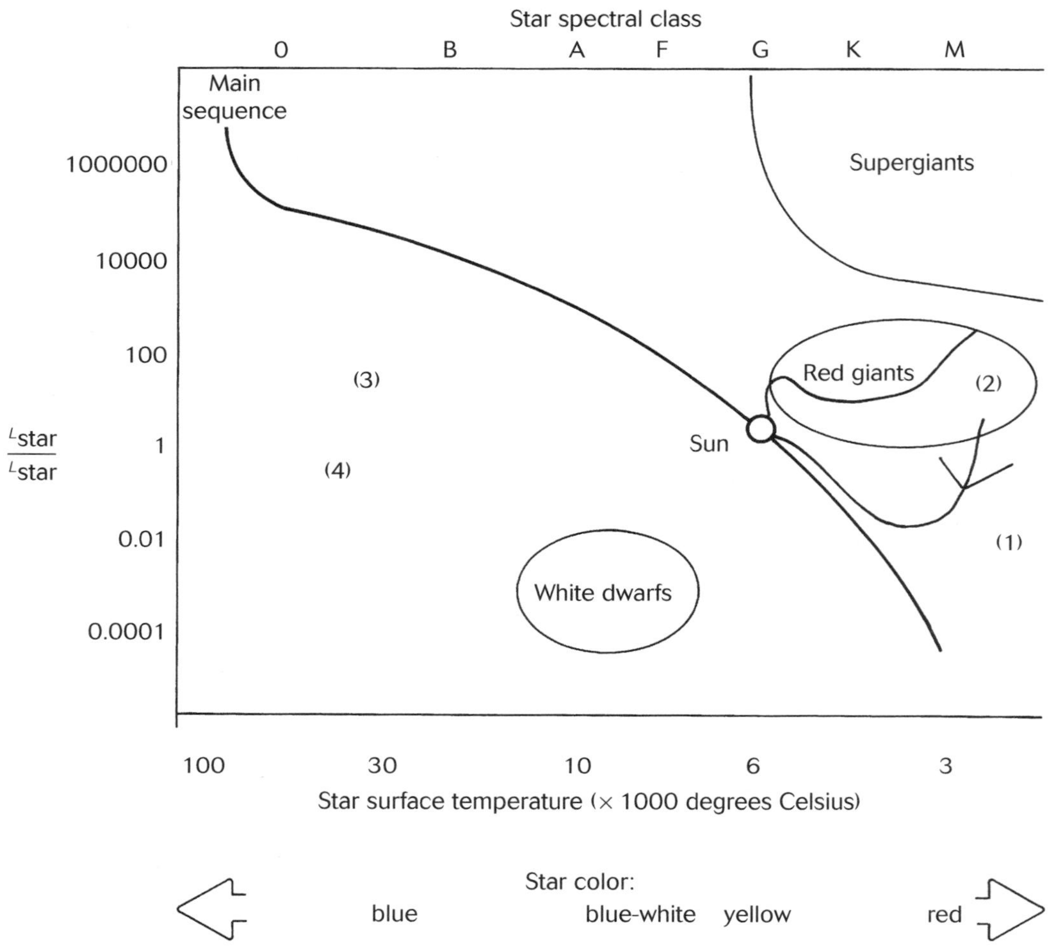

burnt-out stars just visible by the light released when gas layers fall toward the star core are called *white dwarfs*.

About five billion years ago, the infant Sun entered the middle-right side of the HR diagram (position 1 in Figure 7-1). Over the next 100 million years or so, the Sun contracted to the main sequence. Our Sun is about halfway through its life as a hydrogen-burning, main-sequence star. In five billion years or so, it will expand again to become a giant star (position 2). After burning itself out in another 100 million years or so, the Sun will leave the giant phase, cross the main sequence again, and continue contracting (positions 3 and 4) to end its career as a white dwarf.

The Titanic Supernova

Stars many times the mass of our Sun have a more dramatic late career. Starting as O or B stars on the main sequence, they expand after an interval of millions of years to the supergiant phase as shown in the HR diagram. After a supergiant star exhausts much of its nuclear fuel reserves, it begins contracting toward the white dwarf phase.

But the contracting layers of the massive star rapidly raise the temperature in the nuclear furnace in the stellar interior. As the temperature rises, more energetic nuclear reactions occur in the star's interior. The star may convert 1 percent of its mass into energy in a titanic eruption called a *supernova*.

In a typical galaxy like our Milky Way, a supernova occurs about once every century. During the few weeks that a supernova shines brightly, it may outshine all the stars in its home galaxy combined.

During the supernova eruption, much of the star's mass is ejected into space as an expanding nebula of hot gas. In the center of the nebula is the core of the doomed star, which may contract past the white dwarf phase to become a neutron star or a black hole. A *neutron star* is like a giant atomic nucleus, with all the star's mass compacted within a few kilometers. A *black hole* is still smaller, and so dense that even light cannot escape it.

Binary and Multiple Stars

Unlike our Sun, which is isolated in space, most stars are part of *binary* (double) or *multiple star* systems. Astronomers have learned a great deal about star masses by observing the orbits of binary stars. Some binary stars are so aligned that the members of the pair can be viewed to eclipse one another. Observation of these *eclipsing binary* stars has taught astronomers a great deal about star sizes. Binary and other multiple star systems probably form in the crowded confines of the stellar nurseries. The members of a binary system orbit their *center of mass* (the point at which their combined mass is centered) rather than each other.

In some binary star systems, the separation between stars is so great that both members of the pair can be observed visually through the eyepiece of a telescope. Some binaries have closer orbits and can be detected spectroscopically by the shifting spectral lines emitted by the hot gases in the stars' outer layers. Others are so close that they can only be detected by the wobble of the combined image of the two stars.

ACTIVITY 7-1

Observing Some Colorful Binary Stars

To find some interesting binary stars, first become acquainted with the seasonal finder charts in Appendix E. Then use these or a planisphere to locate constellations in the sky such as the ones shown in the binary star finder charts presented as Figures 7-2 through 7-5. The next step is to use the finder charts to locate the binaries in the sky and observe them through your telescope. See the descriptions in this section for specific details to observe.

The four binaries considered here have different colors and angular separations. They are observable during different seasons.

Mizar and Alcor

Certainly the most familiar of binary stars, Mizar and Alcor (also called Zeta Ursae Majoris) are visible as the second star in the handle of the Big Dipper (see Figure 7-2). Both members of this pair are white. Mizar's visible apparent magnitude is 2.4. The dimmer member of the pair, Alcor, has an apparent magnitude of 4.0. These stars currently have an angular separation of about 12 minutes.

Binoculars or a low-power eyepiece are sufficient to visually separate Mizar and Alcor, even under less than ideal skies. In excellent viewing conditions, some people with perfect eyesight have been able to resolve this pair with their unassisted eyes.

Figure 7-2. *Finder chart for Mizar and Alcor.*

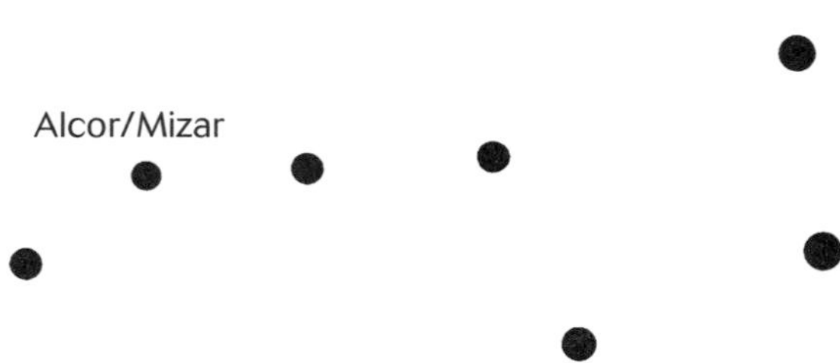

Mizar/Alcor in constellation Ursa Major

As part of the Big Dipper, Mizar and Alcor are always in the sky in midnorthern latitudes. They are highest in early evening skies during late summer or early autumn, about midway between the northern horizon and the zenith.

Rigel

During winter and spring evenings in midnorthern latitudes, the constellation Orion is prominent in the southwestern sky. Rigel (also called Beta Orionis) is a blue-white double marking one of the legs of Orion, the Hunter (see Figure 7-3). Giant Rigel appears white to the human eye and is one of the brightest stars in the sky, with an apparent magnitude of 0.3. Its bluish companion has an apparent magnitude of 6.8. The two members of this pair are separated by only about 10 seconds of arc. Viewing the dimmer member of this pair is a challenge because of the extreme closeness of the two stars and the glare of the primary. Under typical sky conditions, you will probably need a telescope aperture of 15 cm to resolve this pair.

Figure 7-3. *Finder chart for Rigel.*

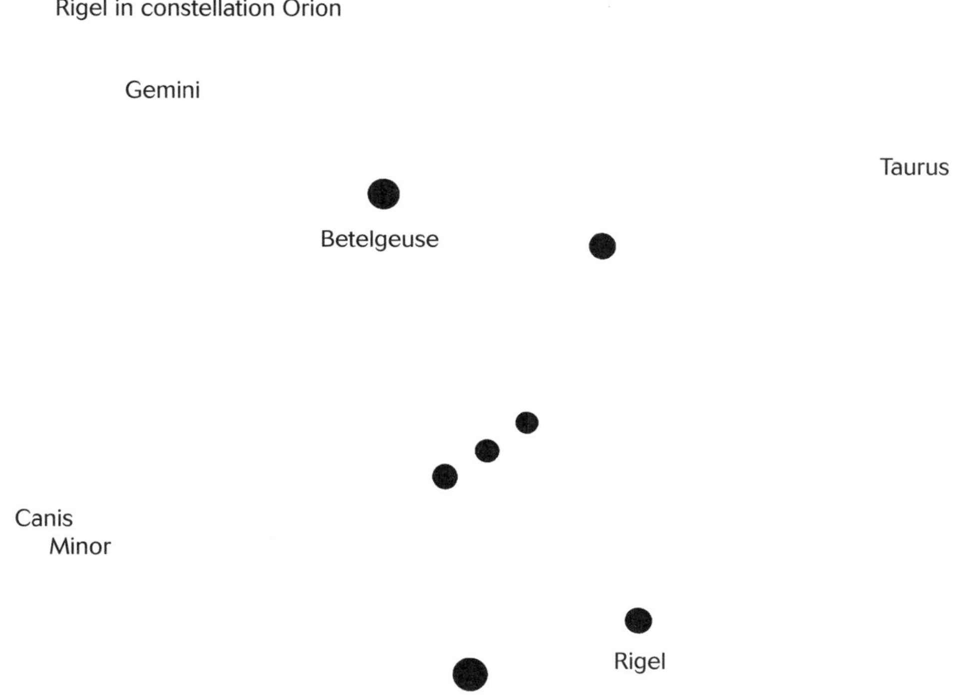

Albireo

Also know as Beta Cygni, Albireo (see Figure 7-4) is best observed in midlatitudes on evenings during early autumn, when it is close to the zenith. It can also be viewed high in the northeastern sky during summer evenings and in the northwest during early winter. Albireo's brighter, orange companion has an apparent magnitude of 3.2; the dimmer member of the pair is blue and has a magnitude of 5.4. The members of this binary are separated by 34 seconds. Many consider Albireo to be the most beautiful of all binaries because of the contrasting colors.

Figure 7-4. *Finder chart for Albireo.*

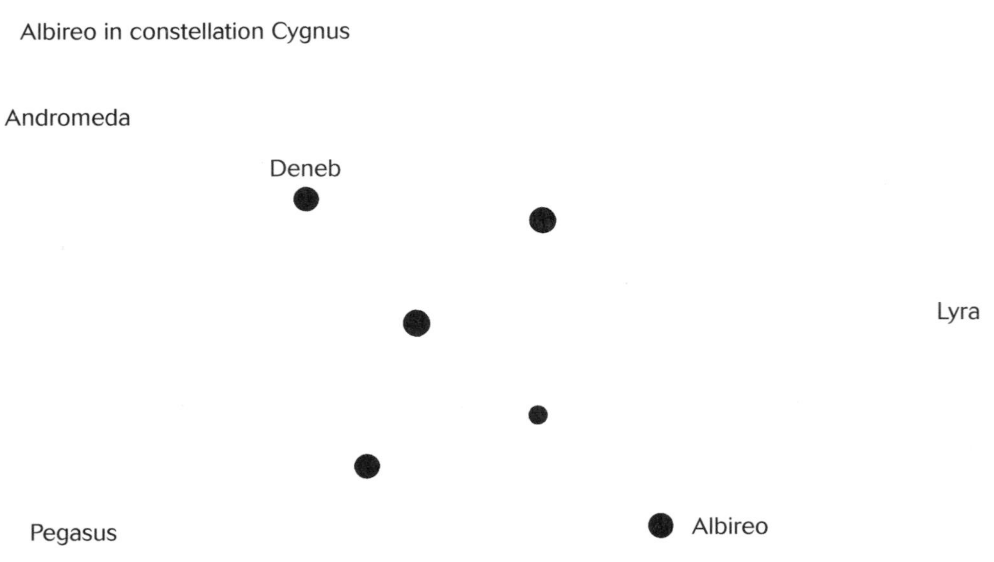

Castor

Castor, also known as Alpha Geminorum, is one of the Gemini Twins (see Figure 7-5). If you observe from midnorthern latitudes, the constellation Gemini is near the zenith on late winter or early spring evenings. The two visual components of Castor are both white and are nearly equal in brightness, with apparent magnitudes of 1.9 and 2.9. Separated by 4 seconds, this pair can be resolved only by telescopes with apertures of 7.5 cm or greater.

Both of the bright members of Castor are themselves spectroscopic binaries. Another close binary, much fainter than the easily observable members of this star system, is also part of Castor.

Figure 7-5. *Finder chart for Castor.*

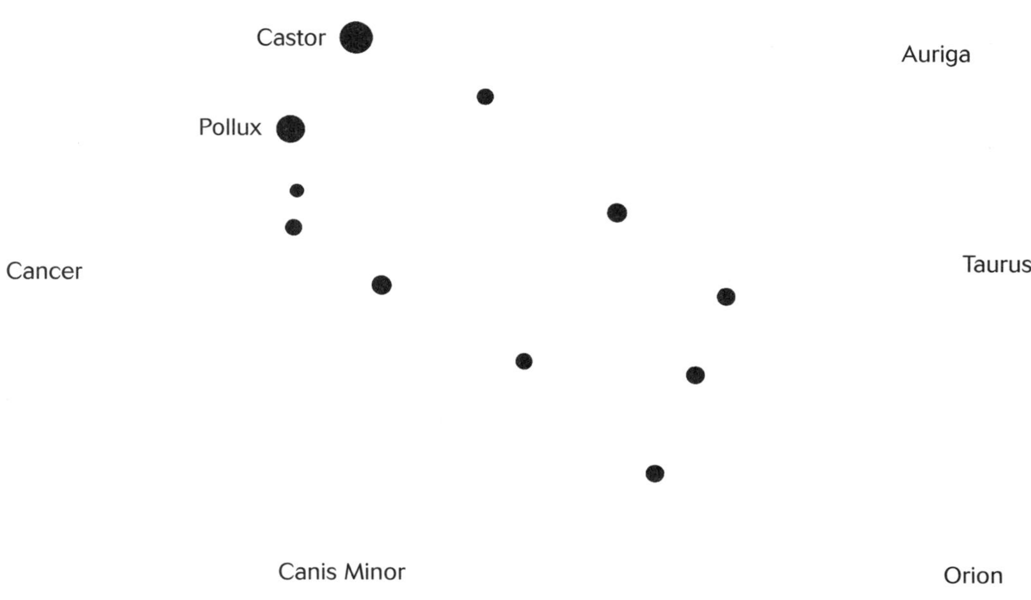

ACTIVITY 7-2

Reticle Observations of Binary Stars

Use a reticle eyepiece to compare the angular separation of binary stars to the Moon's angular diameter. Use your comparisons to estimate the separation of the binary members. How does your estimate for Mizar and Alcor compare with the value given above?

ACTIVITY 7-3

Color-Filter Observations of Binary Stars

Use your color filters to determine colors of binary stars as closely as possible. A red star will seem brightest through a red filter, a blue star through a blue filter. Use the HR diagram in Figure 7-1 to estimate surface temperatures for the members of the binary star system you are observing.

Variable Stars

Variable stars are those that vary in brightness with time. Some of these are eclipsing binaries in which one member passes in front of its partner; others are pulsating variables. One easily observed variable is Polaris, the North Star, in Ursa Minor. This star of the Cepheid type varies between apparent magnitude 2.6 and 2.8 over a period of about four days.

Another easily observed variable is Betelgeuse, also known as Alpha Orionis. At maximum brightness, this star has an apparent magnitude of 0.1. The minimum brightness of this red giant is about 1.2, and the period of variablity is about 2,000 days.

Observation of variable stars requires a great deal of patience, but it can be rewarding. One approach often used by astronomers is to compare a variable star's brightness to stars near it in the sky. The human eye is good enough to detect differences of 0.1 magnitude, which is about 10 percent in the radiant output of a star.

Deep-Sky Objects

Deep-sky objects are objects other than individual stars in the far reaches of the universe, such as nebulae, star clusters, and galaxies. Within our galaxy there are many *nebulae* (clouds of interstellar gas) and *star clusters* (tightly packed associations of many stars) that are readily observable with small telescopes. In *Telescope Power* (Wiley, 1993), I discuss observing some of them, including a star nursery in Orion called the Great Nebula (M42), a *globular cluster* of old stars in Hercules (M13), and the Ring Nebula in Lyra (M57), the remnant of a post-main-sequence star.

ACTIVITY 7-4

Observing M42 through Color Filters

One of the most colorful deep-sky objects is M42, the stellar nursery in Orion called the Great Nebula. You can find this object using the finder chart in Figure 7-6. The fluorescent blue-green color of this nebula is due to the light of infant stars encased in clouds of gas. Use different filters to observe M42. Which filter gives the best image?

Figure 7-6. *Finder chart for M42, the Great Nebula.*

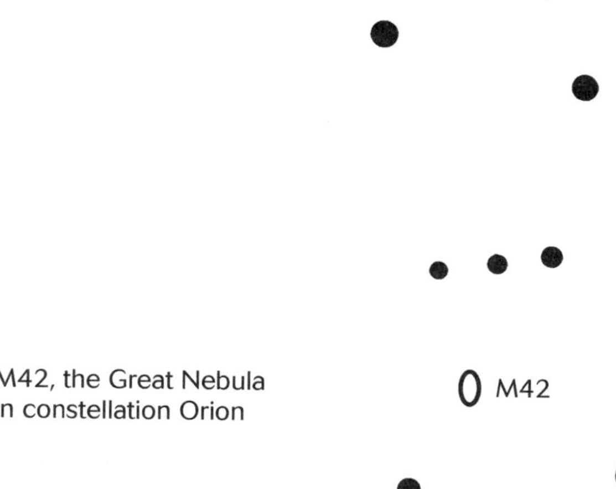

ACTIVITY 7-5

Counting the Pleiades

One deep-sky object that can be observed with the unassisted eye, binoculars, or small telescopes is the star cluster M45, the Pleiades. Located in the constellation Taurus, this collection of young stars can be found with the aid of the the finder chart in Figure 7-7. This cluster is best observed from midnorthern latitudes on evenings from late fall to early spring high in the western sky.

To the ancients, the Pleiades were the Seven Sisters because sharp-eyed observers could count seven members of this cluster. Try observing the Pleiades through successively higher magnifications and count the number of stars visible. There are many more than seven sisters.

Figure 7-7. *Finder chart for M45, the Pleiades.*

M45 (the Pleiades) in constellation Taurus

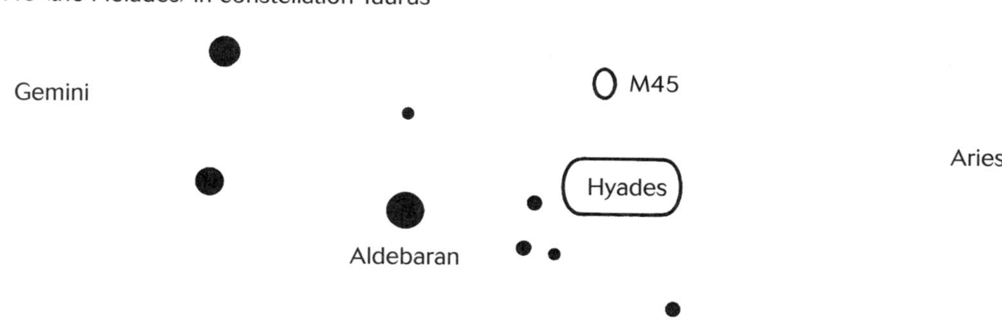

ACTIVITY 7-6

The Milky Way Galaxy and M31, the Great Spiral Galaxy in Andromeda

Our Milky Way Galaxy is a collection of about 100 billion stars arranged in a spiral pattern. Other galaxy types are elliptical (roughly egg shaped) and irregular. You may wish to repeat a similar experiment performed by Galileo and other early astronomers. Point your telescope toward the nearest spiral arm of our galaxy, the Milky Way. Under high magnification, many more stars are visible than to the unassisted eye or binoculars.

Beyond our galaxy are billions of other galaxies, each containing billions of stars. One of these, the Great Spiral Galaxy (M31), in the constellation Andromeda, is visible to the naked eye as a diffuse cloudlike structure. From midlatitudes, M31 is near the zenith on November evenings. Use the finder chart in Figure 7-8 to locate it. There are more than 100 billion stars in M31, which is approximately 2,000,000 light-years away.

Figure 7-8. *Finder chart for M31, the Great Spiral Galaxy.*

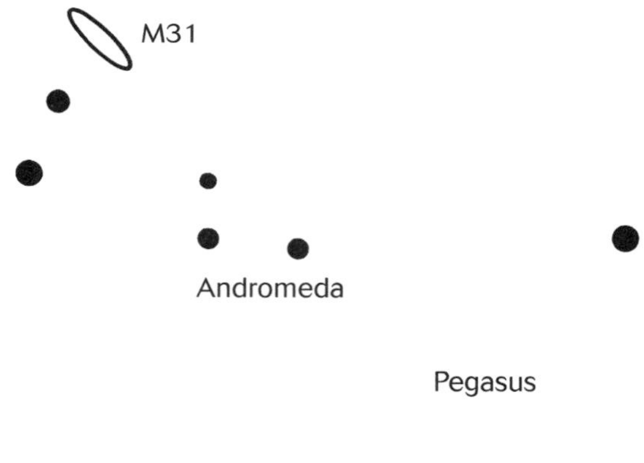

M31 is a relatively near galaxy. Light from the most distant galaxies in the observable universe began its long journey toward Earth billions of years before our solar system originated.

With a small telescope, M31 is about as far as you can easily probe into the depths of intergalactic space. But using the Hubble Space Telescope and other large telescopes, astronomers have found that our universe contains billions of galaxies, each containing billions of stars. With future instruments that will surpass Hubble, we will look back in time close to the origin of the universe and observe planets orbiting nearby stars. Perhaps we will obtain astronomical proof that some of these distant worlds bear life.

APPENDIX A

A Note About Measurement

The United States is one of the few countries still using the English system of distance measurement (inches, feet, and miles). This has resulted in many difficulties, most notably the recent loss of a Mars probe because of a distance conversion error. All distance units in this book are therefore in the more universal metric system. The following table lists some distance conversions:

Metric Conversions

1 kilometer	= 1,000 meters
1 meter	= 100 centimeters
1 meter	= 1,000,000 microns
1 centimeter	= 10 millimeters
1 inch	= 2.54 centimeters
1 foot	= 0.305 meters
1 mile	= 1.609 kilometers

Astronomical Units

Objects in space are usually separated by millions or billions of kilometers. To measure distances within the solar system, astronomers usually use the astronomical unit (abbreviated AU), which is the average distance between the Earth and the Sun. In the vaster galactic and intergalactic realms, they use the light-year, the distance that light moving at 300,000 km per second (186,000 miles per second) travels in one year. The following formulas convert these to familiar units:

1 astronomical unit	=	150,000,000 kilometers	=	93 million miles
1 light-year	=	63,290 astronomical units		

Mass and Weight

The metric system uses mass instead of weight in calculating the amount of material in an object. *Mass* is a measure of the resistance of a body to changes in its motion. The basic units of mass are the gram and the kilogram (1,000 g). This can be converted to the Earth weight of an object in pounds, the gravitational attraction that the Earth exerts on an object near its surface.

1 pound = 454 grams
1 kilogram = 2.205 pounds

Force is defined as the product of mass and acceleration. Weight is a special type of force in which the acceleration is caused by a gravitational field (such as that of the Earth). The unit of force or weight in the metric system is the newton:

1 newton = 0.2247 pounds

Angular Measure

Angular units are degrees, minutes, and seconds. Astronomers sometimes refer to these as degrees, minutes, or seconds of arc to avoid confusion with units of temperature or time.

1 full circle = 360 degrees
1 degree = 60 minutes
1 minute = 60 seconds

APPENDIX B

How to Use a Reticle Eyepiece

Many of the exercises in this book apply the *reticle eyepiece*. This is an eyepiece with an illuminated calibration grid. If you purchase such an eyepiece, you can use it to determine angular separation or size of celestial objects.

Let's say your eyepiece has a field of view (FOV) of 1° and the illuminated grid divides the FOV into four equal parts. Each part has an angular size of 0.25°, or 15 minutes. The full Moon has an angular extent of about 0.5°, so it will fill one half of this hypothetical reticle eyepiece, or two grid divisions.

APPENDIX C

Lunar and Solar Eclipse Table

LUNAR AND SOLAR ECLIPSES

Type of Eclipse	*Date*	*Location*
Total Lunar	Jan. 9, 2001	Africa, Asia, Europe
	May 15, 2003	Americas, Antarctica
	Nov. 8, 2003	Americas
	May 4, 2004	Africa, Middle East, India
	Oct. 27, 2004	Americas, Africa, Europe
	Mar. 3, 2007	Americas, Europe, Africa, Asia
	Aug. 28, 2007	Asia, Australia, Pacific, N. America
	Feb. 21, 2008	Pacific, N. America, Europe, Africa
	Dec. 21, 2010	Asia, Australia, Pacific, N. America, Europe
Total Solar	June 21, 2001	Africa
	Dec. 4, 2002	Africa
	Nov. 23, 2003	Antartica
	Mar. 29, 2006	Africa, S. America
	Aug. 1, 2008	Greenland, Russia, China
	July 11, 2010	S. Pacific, S. America

Sources:

K. Graun, *What's Out Tonight?* (Tucson, AZ: Ken Press, 1999).
www.earthview.com/timetable/future.htm
enchantedlearning.com/subjects/astronomy/Moon/Lunareclipse.shtml
sunearth.gsfc.nasa.gov/eclipse/LEcat/LEbrief2.html

Please consult other sources or monthly astronomy magazines for exact times and path of eclipses.

APPENDIX D

Planet Data Table

PLANET DATA TABLE

Planet	*Distance from Sun (average)*	*Rotation Rate*	*Revolution Rate*	*Mass/Diameter (relative to Earth)*		*Number of Satellites*
Mercury	0.39 AU	58.6 days	0.24 years	0.055	0.38	0
Venus	0.72	–243*	0.62	0.82	0.95	0
Earth	1.00	1	1	1.0	1.00	1
Mars	1.52	1.03	1.88	0.11	0.53	2
Jupiter	5.2	0.41	11.86	317.9	11.21	16
Saturn	9.54	0.44	29.46	95.2	9.45	18
Uranus	19.19	–0.72	84.01	14.5	4.01	17
Neptune	30.06	0.67	164.8	17.1	3.88	8
Pluto	39.53	–6.39	248.6	0.0025	0.18	1

Source: E. Chaisson and S. McMillan, *Astronomy Today*, 3rd ed. (Upper Saddle River, NJ: Prentice Hall, 1999).

*A negative rotation rate means that the planet rotates and revolves in opposite directions.

APPENDIX E

Seasonal Finder Charts

These finder charts show some celestial objects visible in the evening from midnorthern latitudes. To use these charts, hold them overhead with "North" oriented toward compass direction north.

The winter chart (Figure E-1) works best in February between 8:00 and 9:00 P.M.

Figure E-1. *Winter finder chart.*

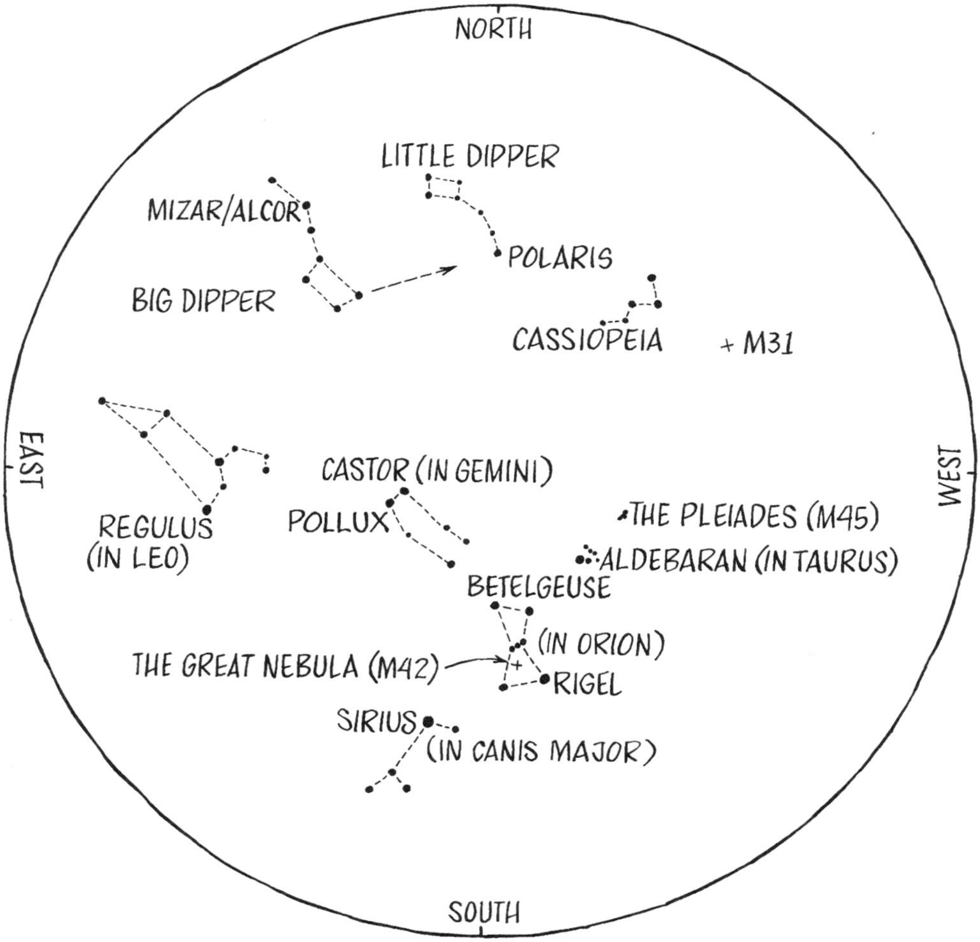

The spring chart (Figure E-2) works best in April between 8:00 and 9:00 P.M.

Figure E-2. *Spring finder chart.*

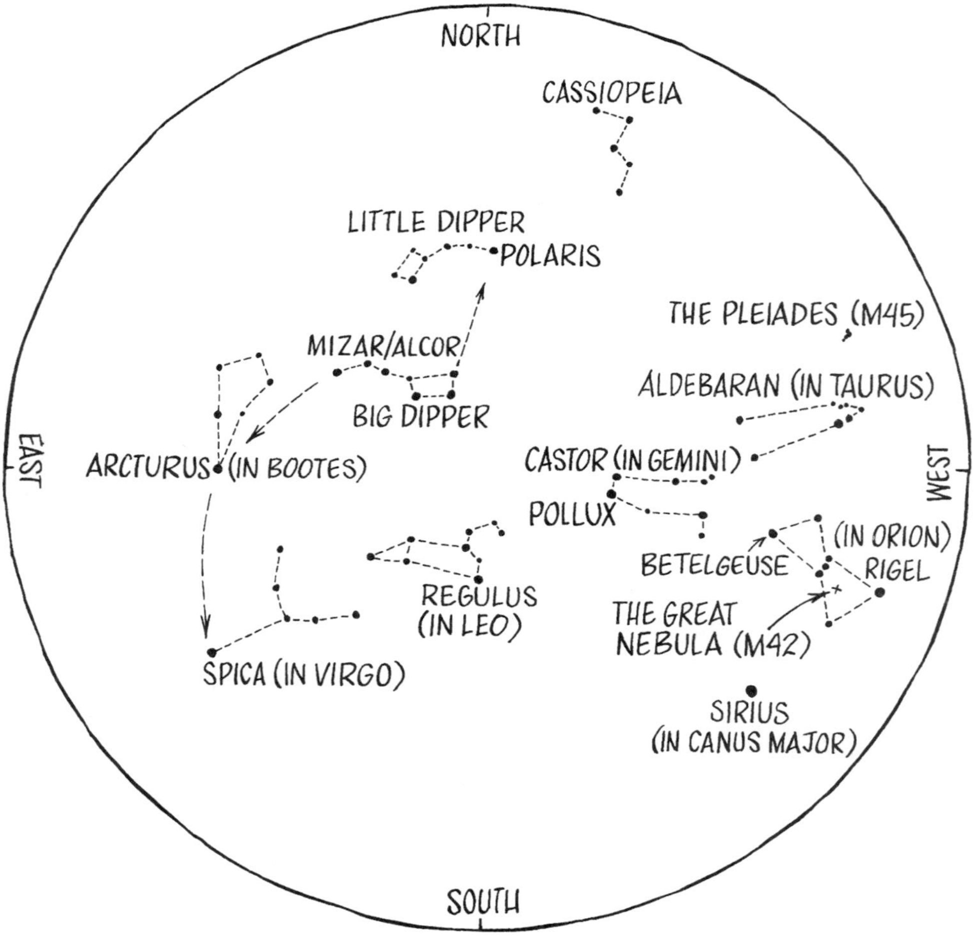

The summer chart (Figure E-3) works best in July between 9:00 and 10:00 P.M.

Figure E-3. *Summer finder chart.*

The autumn chart (Figure E-4) works best in November between 8:00 and 9:00 P.M.

Figure E-4. *Autumn finder chart.*

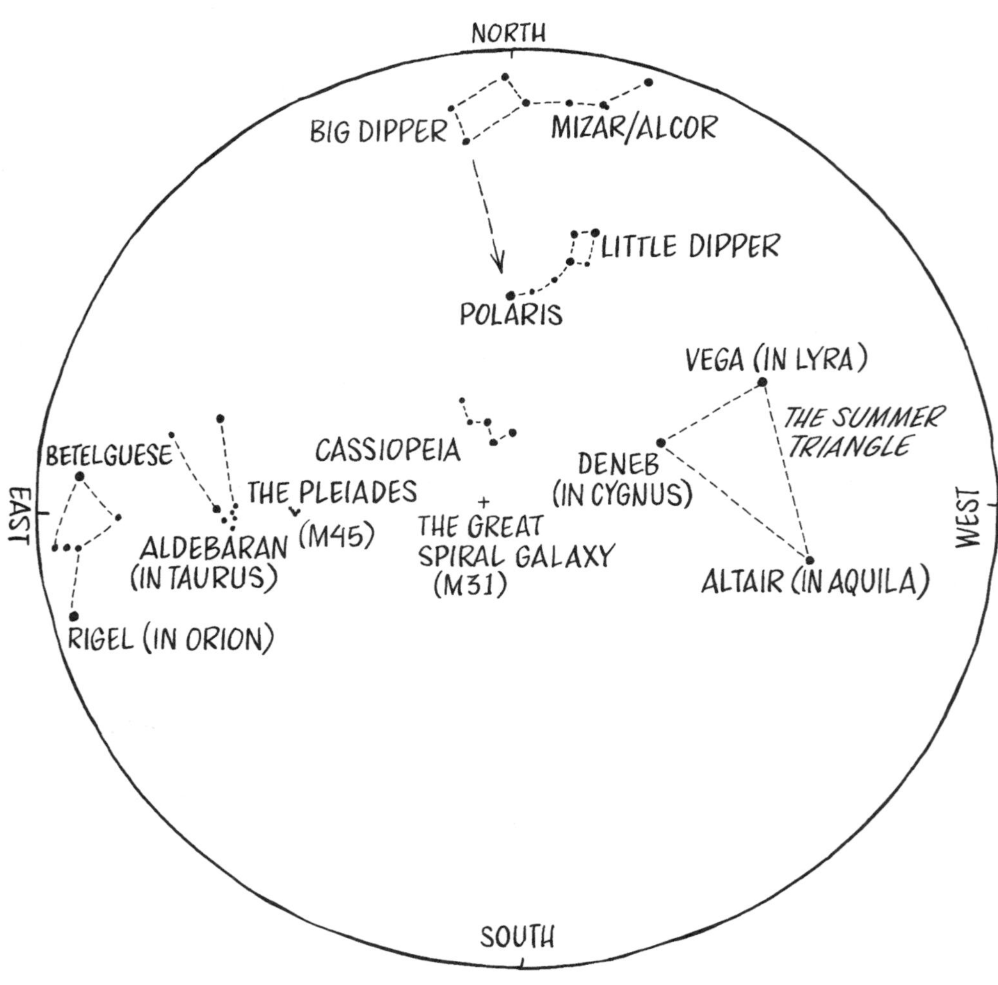

Source: G. L. Matloff, *Telescope Power* (New York: Wiley, 1993).

Reading List: To Dig Deeper

To gain more information about the topics we've discussed, you might wish to consult the following publications. Monthly astronomy magazines such as *Astronomy* and *Sky & Telescope* are also good reference sources.

For Young Astronomers

Gamow, G., and R. Stannard. *The New World of Mr. Tompkins*. New York: Cambridge University Press, 1998.
Gardner, R. *Projects in Space Science*. New York: Simon & Schuster, 1988.
Jobb, J. *The Night Sky Book*. Boston: Little, Brown, 1977.
Matloff, G. L. *Telescope Power*. New York: Wiley, 1993.
Mitton, J. *Zoo in the Sky*. Washington, D.C.: National Geographic Society, 1998.
Moche, D. *Astronomy Today*. New York: Random House, 1977.
Pierce, J. N. *Elementary Astronomy: A Simple Reference Guide to Our Solar System*. Torrance, CA: Good Apple, 2000.
Ride, S., and O. Okie. *To Space and Back*. New York: Lothrup, Lee, & Shepard, 1986.
VanCleave, J. *Astronomy for Every Kid*. New York: Wiley, 1991.
Wiese, J. *Cosmic Science*. New York: Wiley, 1997.

Handbooks, Guides, and Atlases

de Grasse Tyson, N., C. Liu, and R. Irion. *One Universe*, Washington, D.C.: J. Henry, 2000.
Foust, J., and R. Lafon. *Astronomer's Computer Companion* (electronic book). San Francisco: No Starch Press, 1999.
Graun, K. *What's Out Tonight?* Tucson, AZ: Ken Press, 1999.
Harrington, P. S. *Star Ware*. New York: Wiley, 1994.
Kepple, G. R., and G. W. Sanner, eds. *The Night Sky Observer's Guide*. Richmond, VA: Willman-Bell, 1998.
Maron, S. B. *Astronomy for Dummies*. New York: IDG Books, 1999.
Matloff, G. L. *The Urban Astronomer*. New York: Wiley, 1991.

Monkhouse, R., and J. Cox. *3D Atlas of Stars and Galaxies*. London: Springer-Verlag, 2000.

Mosley, J. *Stargazing with Binoculars and Telescopes*. New York: Barnes & Noble, 2000.

Roth, G. D. *Stars and Planets: A Viewer's Guide*. New York: Sterling, 1998.

Tirion, W., and R. W. Sinnott. *Sky Atlas 2000*, 2nd ed. New York: Sky Publishing and Cambridge University Press, 1998.

Upgren, A. *Night Has a Thousand Eyes*. New York: Plenum, 1998.

Annuals

The Astronomical Almanac. Washington, D.C.: Nautical Almanac Office, U.S. Naval Observatory.

Astronomical Calendar. Guy Ottewell, ed. Greenville, S.C.: Furman University.

Astronomical Yearbook. Melbourne, Australia: Astronomical Society of Victoria.

Observer's Handbook. Toronto: Royal Astronomical Society of Canada.

Glossary

absolute magnitude: A measure of star brightness that compensates for star distance (compare with *apparent magnitude*).

acceleration: The rate at which an object's velocity changes with time.

annular eclipse: A solar eclipse occurring when the Moon is near apogee and a ring of sunlight is visible around the lunar disk.

aperture: The effective diameter of an optical system.

aphelion: The farthest point from the Sun in a celestial body's orbit.

apogee: The farthest point from Earth in an Earth satellite's orbit.

apparent magnitude: A measure of star brightness that does not correct for star distance (compare with *absolute magnitude*).

apparition: A comet's visit to the inner solar system.

asteroid: A minor planet. Most minor planets orbit between Mars and Jupiter.

astronomical unit: The average Earth–Sun separation, about 150,000,000 km.

aurora: A display of lights caused by the interaction of solar wind and Earth's upper atmosphere in Earth's magnetic field; commonly called northern lights, or aurora borealis, and southern lights, or aurora australis.

binary (multiple) star: A star system with two (or more) members.

black hole: A celestial object so dense that light cannot escape it.

bolide: An exceptionally bright meteor trail; commonly called a fireball.

brown dwarf: A celestial object intermediate in size between a planet and a star.

center of mass: The point at which the combined mass of a system is centered.

Cepheid variable: A pulsating variable whose pulsation rate depends upon radiant output.

chromosphere: The lower atmospheric layer of the Sun.

coma: A large sphere of evaporated ice surrounding the nucleus of a comet.

comet: A small (20–30 km) solar-system body consisting of layers of dust, ice, and rock.

cometoid: A cometlike body larger than a comet but smaller than most planets.

conic sections: A method of generating circles, ellipses, parabolas, and hyperbolas from a cone.

constellation: A convenient star pattern.

corona: The upper atmospheric layer of the Sun.

cosmic ray: A high-energy electrically charged particle accelerated by celestial magnetic fields.

cosmogony: A model of the solar system.

deep-sky object: Any distant nonstellar celestial object.

density: The measure of mass per unit volume.

eclipse: A celestial event occurring when one celestial body passes in front of another, from the point of view of a terrestrial observer.

eclipsing binary: A binary star whose members eclipse each other.

ecliptic: The apparent path of the Sun and major planets across the sky.

electromagnetic radiation: Radiation that is propagated by variations in electric or magnetic fields and that moves at 300,000 km/sec, the velocity of light.

emission nebula: A nebula shining by the light of infant stars.

energy: The ability to do work (work = force × displacement).

epicycle: An apparent loop in a planet's path through the sky caused by relative motions of the planet and Earth around the Sun.

eyepiece: The lens of a telescope that directs light to the observer's eye.

field of view (FOV): The angular fraction of the sky that can be viewed at any one time through a telescope.

filter: A device that reduces the amount of light passing through a telescope.

focal length: The distance between a lens (or a mirror) and the focus.

focus: The point where optical rays from a distant light source converge.

force: The product of an object's mass and acceleration.

galaxy: A grouping of billions of stars.

gas giant: See *Jovian planet*.

geocentric model: A solar-system model in which the Moon, the Sun, and the planets orbit the Earth.

geosynchronous Earth orbit (GEO): An artificial Earth-satellite orbit such that the satellite revolves at the same rate as the Earth rotates. The satellite tends to stay over the same spot on the Earth.

giant star: A class of large, bright stars.

globular cluster: See *star cluster*.

heliocentric model: A solar-system model in which the planets orbit the Sun.

Hertzsprung-Russell (HR) diagram: A characterization of many star properties, including brightness, size, and color.

hyperbola: A conic section in which the ends diverge.

inertia: The tendency of an object to resist changes of its motion.

inferior planet: A planet closer to the Sun than the Earth is.

infrared: A form of electromagnetic radiation lower in energy than red visible light.

Jovian planet: A large planet with a dense atmosphere, many satellites, and a ring system; also called *gas giant*.

Kuiper belt: A region between 30 and 50 astronomical units from the Sun that is populated by many cometoids.

light-gathering power (LGP): The ability of a telescope to make a dim object seem brighter.

low earth orbit (LEO): The location of most artificial Earth satellites, a few hundred kilometers above Earth's surface.

magnification: Making a small object seem larger.

main-sequence star: A hydrogen-burning star.

mare (pl: maria): A comparatively smooth, dark region of the lunar surface.

mass (*m*): A measure of the total amount of material in a body.

meteor: A tiny piece of ice or dust, usually from a comet's tail, that burns up in Earth's upper atmosphere; commonly called a "shooting star."

meteorite: An object from space that survives pasasage through the Earth's atmosphere and hits our planet's surface.

meteoroid: The parent body of a meteor or meteorite.

naked-eye planet: A planet that is visible to the unassisted eye.

nebula: A cloud of interstellar dust, gas, and often stars.

neutrino: A subatomic particle with low or zero mass that is very nonreactive with matter.

neutron star: A collapsed star a few kilometers in diameter.

nuclear fusion zone: See *thermonuclear fusion zone*.

objective lens: The major optical element of a refracting telescope.

occultation: A celestial event occurring when a celestial object passes behind another celestial object of greater angular extent.

Oort Cloud: A spherical region extending about 100,000 AU from the Sun that is inhabited by billions of comets.

open cluster: See *star cluster*.

opposition: The position of two celestial bodies opposite each other.

parabola: A conic section that is open at one end.

partial eclipse: An eclipse in which one celestial object partially covers another.

penumbra: The less dark, outer region of a sunspot. Also, the shadow cast by the eclipsing body during a partial eclipse.

perigee: The point closest to the Earth in the orbit of an Earth satellite.

perihelion: The closest approach of a celestial body to the Sun.

phases: Changes in apparent shape.

photon: The smallest individual unit of electromagnetic energy.

photosphere: The visible surface of the Sun.

planet: A celestial object orbiting a star and shining by reflected light.

planisphere: An astronomical tool that allows the user to see what's in the sky at a particular time and location.

posigrade motion: The normal direction of planetary motion in the sky.

pressure: A measure of force per unit area.

primary mirror: The major optical element of a reflecting telescope.

protoplanet: A planet in the early stage of its evolution.

protostar: An infant star.

pulsating variable: A star that varies in brightness as it pulsates.

radiant: A point in the sky from which the tracks of a meteor shower originate.

radiation pressure: The push associated with light.

radio: The lowest-frequency waveband of electromagnetic radiation.

reflecting telescope: A telescope that uses a mirror as the primary element.

refract: To bend (light) as it travels from one medium to another.

refracting telescope: A telescope that uses a lens as the primary element.

resolution: The property of a telescope that allows an observer to view fine details of a distant object; also called *resolving power*.

reticle eyepiece: An accessory that allows the user to measure the size or angular separation of celestial objects.

retrograde motion: The occasional backward motion of a planet in the sky.

revolve: To orbit a body, as a planet about its star.

rotate: To spin about an axis.

RR Lyrae variable: A pulsating variable whose pulsation rate depends upon radiant output.

satellite: An object that orbits a planet and shines by reflected light.

secondary mirror: The secondary optical element of a reflecting telescope.

solar flare: An eruption of the Sun's photospheric materials.

solar maximum: A time of maximum solar activity.

solar wind: A stream of electrically charged particles emitted by the Sun.

spectral signature: The characteristic spectrum of a gas.

spectroscope: A device that separates white light into its constituent colors, usually with prisms or diffraction gratings.

spectrum: The colors that comprise white light.

star: A self-luminous celestial object.

star cluster: A grouping of many stars. *Open clusters* contain mostly young stars; *globular clusters* contain older stars.

stellar luminosity class: Division of stars into classification by radiant output. Some of the main stellar luminosity classes are supergiant, giant, main sequence, and white dwarf.

stellar spectral class: Division of stars by color and surface temperature. Starting from hot, blue stars and concluding with cool, red stars, the major spectral classes are O, B, A, F, G, K, and M.

sunspot: A dark-looking region on the Sun that is slightly cooler than the surrounding photosphere.

supergiant: A very large and bright star.

superior planet: A planet farther from the Sun than Earth is.

supernova: A titanic stellar explosion.

telescopic planet: A planet that is only visible through a telescope.

temperature: A measure of the internal energy of an object.

terminator: The boundry between light and dark on the visible surface of a celestial object.

terraform: To make a planet more Earth-like.

terrestrial planet: A comparatively small planet with a rocky surface, a thin atmosphere, and few or no natural satellites.

thermonuclear fusion: A process by which light atomic nuclei combine to release energy.

thermonuclear fusion zone: The region in a star's interior where matter is converted into energy; also called the *nuclear fusion zone*.

tides: The diurnal (daily) variation in the level of Earth's atmosphere caused (mainly) by the Moon. The Earth also produces tides on the Moon.

total eclipse: An eclipse in which one celestial body completely covers another.

trajectory: The path of a spacecraft.

transit: The movement of one celestial object passing in front of another.

umbra: The darker, central region of a sunspot. Also, the shadow cast by the eclipsing body during a total eclipse.

variable star: A star that varies in brightness because of either internal pulsations or a stellar eclipse.

velocity: Distance covered per unit of time.

wane: To become dimmer.

wax: To become brighter.

white dwarf: A collapsed dying star.

zenith: The point in the sky directly overhead.

ziggurat: A tower used in ancient Babylon to observe planetary motions.

Index

Note: Pages with illustrations are given in *italics*.